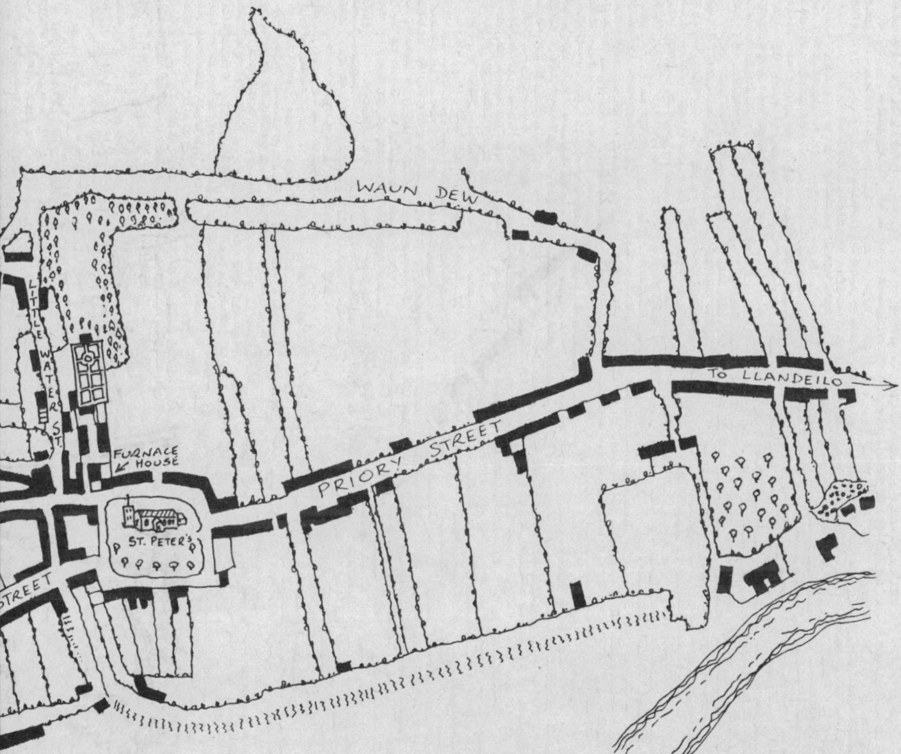

WAUN DEW
LITTLE WATER ST.
FURNACE HOUSE
ST. PETER'S
PRIORY STREET
STREET
TO LLANDEILO

PAT. MOLLOY 1979

# Four Cheers for Carmarthen . . .

the other side of the coin

A TOWN UNIQUE IN WALES

*A Sword-bearer of the Mayor shall freely and lawfully carry the Sword before the said Mayor, in the manner as is accustomed to be done in our City of London (The Carmarthen Town Charter of Henry VIII, 1546)*

No other town in Wales has ever been accorded this privilege, and this is the original sword, still carried before the Mayor after more than four centuries.

# Four Cheers for Carmarthen
## the other side of the coin

Pat Molloy

Gomer Press
1981

*First Impression - December 1981*

ISBN 0 85088 925 1



*Printed by*
*J. D. Lewis and Sons Ltd., Llandysul, Dyfed.*

To Carmarthen, and to
all my friends there.

## ACKNOWLEDGEMENTS

The author once again acknowledges all the help he received during his research for this book and its companion, *A Shilling for Carmarthen.* Although most of the material had already been collected, the preparation for publication of *Four Cheers for Carmarthen* entailed further calls on the staffs of the Dyfed Archive Service, the Dyfed County Library at Carmarthen, the National Library of Wales and the Public Record Office, all of which were met with the same unfailing courtesy. He also thanks Mr. Bill Adey of Cardigan for his contribution, not used until now.

For the illustrations used here, and for their kind permission to use them, the author also thanks the National Army Museum, the Swansea Maritime and Industrial Museum, the National Library of Wales, the Town Clerk of Carmarthen, the author (Mr. Grahame Farr) and the publishers (T. Stephenson and Sons Ltd.) of *West Country Passenger Steamers.* Again, a number of local people lent postcards and photographs, and the author has great pleasure in thanking them here: Mr. Terry James (The Rampart Press), Mr. Ken Davies (Mayfair Studios), Mr. Roy Evans of the Ferryside Residential Centre, Mr. Des Spawton, Mr. Sid Jones, Mr. Peter Thomas, Mrs. Katie Evans, Mrs. Brenda Robinson, Mr. Emlyn Jones, Mr. Theo Rogers, Mrs. Anne Davies (Trevaughan) and Mr. George Davies (Cwmduad).

The author is especially grateful to Mr. Chris Delaney, Curator of Carmarthen Museum, for pictures of his exhibits and for copies of pictures from the Museum's archive collection. And to Mr. David Edmunds, Editor of the *Carmarthen Journal,* in whose files are locked a hundred and seventy years of the life and times of Carmarthen, and who kindly helped the author to unlock some of them. It will surely not escape the reader's notice that a great debt is owed to the Journal in the telling of these stories of Old Carmarthen. In fact, where no other source is shown for material quoted in this book, the source will be the *Carmarthen Journal.*

Finally, the author wishes to thank the two reviewers who reminded him in their reviews of *A Shilling for Carmarthen* that a book is the better for the inclusion of an index. That omission is remedied here. But more than that. For the benefit of those who already possess *A Shilling,* the index covers that, too.

# CONTENTS


| | Page |
|---|---|
| HEROES | 1 |
| The Soldiers' General: Lieutenant General Sir Thomas Picton. | 5 |
| Sergeant John Samuel, Waterloo Medal. | 20 |
| The Sepoy General: Major General Sir William Nott. | 21 |
| Sergeant Major Kyle of the 41st. | 28 |
| Crimea | 31 |
| Private David Thomas, 4th Light Dragoons. | 34 |
| Soldiers of the Queen: The volunteer Saint Peter's Boys. | 37 |
| A Soldier's Life | 49 |
| CARRIAGES | 59 |
| The Iron Road. | 65 |
| The Mighty Power of Steam. | 74 |
| SHIPS | 89 |
| 'This Town cannot do without a Steamer.' | 116 |
| CONTRASTS | 131 |
| Two Nations. | 132 |
| Arrivals. | 155 |
| The gulf narrows. | 172 |
| Towards the Threshold. | 197 |
| The flight of industry. | 202 |
| What strides. | 207 |

# PREFACE

My book *A Shilling for Carmarthen*[1] employed only about a third of my original manuscript, which was the product of three years research. It was a compromise dictated by today's high cost of publishing and, inevitably, something was lost along the way. That book, with its theme of the development of law and order in the nineteenth century, highlighted just one aspect of the most far-reaching social upheaval in British history. Of necessity, the dominance of that central theme often allowed the less strident melodies of the colourful symphony which was life in nineteenth century Carmarthen to be at the most only tantalisingly heard and at the least merely hinted at. This volume, intended as a companion to *A Shilling for Carmarthen,* draws on the remainder of my material and, I hope, fills out the orchestration.

Turbulence, violence, corruption and drunkenness there certainly were, but the volatility of the people of Carmarthen also found other, happier, outlets. And though poverty and distress plagued the 'Lower Orders' of Carmarthen for the greater part of the century, most of its inhabitants were too preoccupied with the business of making a living—or of merely existing—to join the noisy minority that figured so prominently in the story of the 'Carmarthen Shilling'. This is their story. And as for the town itself, we shall look now at its changing character as the industrial revolution eroded its importance, as the railway train supplanted the stage coach and the steamer the sailing ship. We shall see how the ending of Carmarthen's comparative isolation combined with the spread of education and other civilising influences to bring a kind of order to an inherently uninhibited town.

This book is different in another way. It has no central theme, but is divided into four parts, each with its own theme of change and progress in just one facet of life in nineteenth century Carmarthen. 'Heroes' looks at what lies behind Carmarthen's unusual collection of military monuments; 'Carriages' at the transition from stagecoach to railway;

'Ships' at the rise and decline of the port of Carmarthen, and 'Contrasts' at some of the achievements of the nineteenth century as they affected, and improved, the lives of ordinary people. They are the four stories that, to me at least, evoke the feel of the nineteenth century in a town that has more character than any other I know.

*Carmarthen—June, 1981* PAT MOLLOY

NOTE

[1] *A Shilling for Carmarthen . . . The Town they Nearly Tamed,* published 1980 by Gomer Press, Llandysul, Dyfed. The term 'Shilling' was applied to the Carmarthen Borough Police Force, consisting as it did of twelve "coppers".

# Heroes

''When some Lord or General or Colonel has been killed or wounded, fame takes her trumpet and sounds it through the world. But who shall record the glorious deeds of the soldier whose lot is numbered with the thousands in the ranks who live and die and fight in obscurity?''

Private William Wheeler (1813)

# HEROES

At just after noon on Wednesday the 13th of November, 1805, the Swansea coach sped down Llangunnor Hill, its rear wheels streaming mud from the rain-soaked, rutted, earthen road, and its guard up front straining to push the notes of his long post horn ahead of the rocking conveyance and into nearby Carmarthen town to announce its approach. The whole commotion drowned the words shouted to the scattered groups of country people by the driver, by the muffled and blanketted outside passengers clinging precariously to their swaying perches, and by those inside who, clearly having some message to impart, pulled down the windows and braved the autumn drizzle to do so.

What was the message? What was the news? None could be sure, but the wreaths of evergreens which festooned the Swansea coach as it hurtled over the town bridge to take the run at steep, narrow Bridge Street proclaimed it themselves . . . for this was the traditional way of bringing news of a great victory.

Men dropped their burdens, women hitched up their skirts and ran, and children hallooed with the excitement of it all as they followed the sound of the post horn now fading away towards Carmarthen town. The word spread like wildfire and the hurrying groups of country people were joined by their town neighbours until they swelled to a huge and noisy crowd, which pressed up Bridge Street and Quay Street and into and around King Street, where, at the Ivy Bush coaching inn, the coachman—the only newsbringer in those times—was announcing his tidings: The British fleet had destroyed the combined fleets of France and Spain twenty three days ago, at a place in the eastern Atlantic known as Cape Trafalgar. But resounding cheers quickly gave way to stunned silence as the rest of the news spread through the crowd. Admiral Lord Nelson, the nation's hero, was dead—struck down by a sharpshooter from the mizzen top of the French warship 'Redoutable'. Many in the crowd remembered the great Admiral coming to

Carmarthen, staying in that very inn and attending the King Street theatre with his Lady Hamilton only a year or two before, and so there was that extra sense of loss to mingle with the joy attending the news of the defeat of Old Boney and the removal of the threat of a French invasion.

In no time, the town was festooned with banners and evergreens, and as evening fell it began to glow with oil lamps, bonfires and candle-lit windows for the kind of celebration that brought out all the distinctive exuberance which characterised nineteenth century Carmarthen. For these were the days of Military Glory, the days when war was conducted by manoeuvering hosts of gaudily caparisoned soldiers and great columns of wooden men o' war in places far away; the days before ordinary men could communicate the horror of it all to the people back home, and the days before war touched those people at home, sheltered on their island behind the wooden walls of their great navy. They were the days when the people at home vicariously shared in the thrill of battle and the relief of victory by street celebrations and services of thanksgiving.

Muted though it was by grief, the explosion of popular joy at the news of Trafalgar was still greater than any before experienced in a town renowned for its strength of feeling. The bells of Saint Peter's rang throughout the day and night, alternating its peals of joy with the tolling of a single funereal bell. The crowds sang patriotic songs and fuelled their delight with liberal quantities of the cheap and abundant liquor sold in the hundred and fifty or so licensed alehouses and gin shops and the innumerable unlicensed back street beer parlours. The gentry and better class of tradesmen celebrated well into the night in the coaching inns—in the Red Lion, the Talbot, the Half Moon and the Nag's Head, almost within touching distance of each other at narrow Dark Gate and below the Guildhall, in the Boar's Head[1] in Lammas Street, and, of course, in the chief of them, the Ivy Bush[2] in King Street. Only a few years earlier the French officers captured in the last ever invasion of Britain, at Fishguard forty miles west of Carmarthen, had been housed there, until the Mayor had anxiously petitioned for their removal because of their impact on the local maidens . . . and its landlord had a son named William Nott serving as a young officer in the Bengal Regiment of the

Honourable East India Company, of whom much would be heard in the town in the years to come.

A backdrop to all this was provided by the booming of cannon from the sailing ships tied alongside the quay and anchored on the Towy River, by the crackle and sparkle of fireworks and rockets from the Pensarn bank opposite the steep and crowded terraces of Carmarthen's riverside, and by the inevitable blazing torches and cracking pistols. And the Borough Corporation staged an appropriate tribute to the occasion, so that:

> Carmarthen was most superbly illuminated with a variety of transparencies, devices, &c. indicative of the gallant Nelson's triumph and lamented fall. The Mayor, William Morgan, and the Corporation, who were previously assembled at the Ivy Bush Inn, paraded the town, preceded by the Carmarthen Volunteer Band playing 'God Save the King' and 'Rule Britannia', and occasionally a solemn dirge with drums muffled. When the procession reached a large bonfire which had been made in Market Street,[3] they found several large bowls of punch awaiting their arrival, and a number of patriotic toasts were drunk in copious libations.
>
> Here the scene received additional zest from the appearance of the Carmarthen Volunteers who had been ordered out, together with Captain Bowen's Troop of Horse on duty there, who fired a volley. About ten o'clock, the Corporation &c. returned to the Ivy Bush Inn and devoted the remainder of the evening to agreeable conviviality. (*Cambrian*).

And through the last hours of the night's celebrations, amid all the clamour of his drunken town, old Wil Alone, Carmarthen's only Watchman, peace-keeper and bastion of law and order,[4] sat huddled in his 'Watchbox', snoring away his own "copious libations" and dreaming of the days when he had fought the King's wars in far-off lands, before returning war-weary, wounded and spent by the exertions of a soldier's life, to take up the only job he was fit for.

It was a tired but happy populace that staggered home in the early hours of the next morning, the 'lower orders' to their packed, tiny and insanitary hovels on the quay, along the riverside and in the narrow back streets, and the better off to their town houses in Quay Street and Spilman Street, or by chaise or coach to homes further afield.

For the poor, who formed the greater part of Carmarthen's inhabitants, it had been a chance to escape from the daily struggle to survive, but for everyone in town for that great celebration it had been an opportunity to do that at which the people of Carmarthen excelled . . . to take the trials, tribulations and worries of daily life and throw them to the winds for one mad moment of unrestrained enjoyment. And nothing brought them out onto the streets like a famous victory . . . except the exploits or the triumphal return home of Carmarthen's own heroes.

[1] The last of the old coaching inns, it is still in business.

[2] This was the "Old" Ivy Bush Inn. Another Ivy Bush was built later in the century on the site of the present Ivy Bush Royal Hotel in Spilman Street.

[3] Now Nott Square, above the Guildhall. The old name derives from the market which was removed to a new site in 1846.

[4] A nickname derived from his Welsh name Wil y Lôn (Wil (of) the Lane) and from the loneliness of his job. Britain would not have anything like police forces until the 1830's, and Wil represented the last remnant of a fast-crumbling system of law and order known as "Watch and Ward" created 500 years before. See *A Shilling for Carmarthen,* Chapter 1.

## The Soldiers' General

Lieutenant General Sir Thomas Picton, a Pembrokeshire man, was gazetted as an Ensign in his father's infantry regiment at the incredibly early age of thirteen in 1781. The immense physical courage for which this hard-swearing disciplinarian became famous was demonstrated early in his career when, as a Captain of twenty-five, he fought his way alone into the middle of a rioting mob of mutinous soldiers—a whole regiment—grabbed the ringleader, dragged him out of the throng and beat him into submission. The mutiny was over! Ten years of military adventure in the West Indies sharpened his aggressive spirit and his capacity for leadership, in campaigns against the Spaniards and the suppression of rebellions among slaves and native troops, while his own arrest and an inconclusive trial on a charge of allowing the use of torture almost brought his career to a premature close. Clearly he was no ordinary soldier. Now Lord Wellington's right-hand man in the Peninsular campaign against Napoleon's Marshals, large, physically powerful and of legendary courage, Sir Thomas Picton was taken to the hearts of the people of Carmarthen, in whose town his brother, the Reverend Edward Picton, was a pillar of the establishment.[1] As Lord Wellington's Peninsular Army gained the ascendancy over the French, every dispatch from Spain brought the townspeople onto the streets to cheer the exploits of the Commander-in-Chief's favourite, bravest and most eccentric divisional commander.

On the 2nd of May, 1812, twenty six days after the event, news reached Carmarthen by sailing ship and post coach of Picton's greatest exploit, the capture by storm of the heavily fortified castle at Badajoz in Spain. That ferocious and bloody battle, the background to Picton's portrait now hanging in Carmarthen's Guildhall chamber, almost defies description. Leaving five thousand British and Portugese soldiers dead, the holocaust in the breach of the town walls and the fury of the fight on the forty-foot scaling ladders up which the wounded Picton urged his entire division of four thousand troops to the castle battlements, drove men mad. Such was their post-battle frenzy that they sacked the town and butchered the defenders and inhabitants for three days and nights after their spirited defence had ended. Lord Wellington, the 'Iron Duke', famed for his coolness and lack of emotion, had broken down and cried when he saw the mass of bodies on the glacis, in the breach of the town walls, and at the foot of the scaling ladders. But he soon recovered his composure and ordered the erection of gallows and the hanging of a sufficient number of British soldiers to persuade their comrades that enough was enough and to bring a swift end to the looting and killing.

The Duke's revulsion at the slaughter of the battle was summed up in his dispatch to London, in which he wrote:

> The capture of Badajoz affords as strong an instance of the gallantry of our troops as has ever been displayed, but I anxiously hope that I shall never again be the instrument of putting them to such a test as they were in last night. When I ordered the assault I was certain I should lose our best officers and men. It is a cruel situation for any person to be placed in . . .[2]

Picton's greatest exploit: The storming of Badajoz. *(National Army Museum).*

To have been the hero of that night of heroes is proof enough of the strength and courage of General Picton, but an extract from a letter written by one of Wellington's Staff Officers underlines the fact:

> To describe the attack on Badajoz is beyond my power. No man ever deserved better of his country than General Picton. Had it not been for his skill in the attack he made upon the castle we might still have been on the outside of the town. He is a most extraordinary officer and highly esteemed by the whole army.

Lieutenant General Sir Thomas Picton returned in triumph to Carmarthen in the following November, approaching the town through Llangunnor on the road from Swansea, and being met by a great crowd of cheering townspeople led by the Mayor and the Corporation. At once the horses were removed from the shafts of Picton's carriage and, with his brother the Rev. Edward Picton and the Borough's Member of Parliament, John Jones of Ystrad, he was pulled by the aid of long ropes, by the shouting, singing, banner-waving crowd. Up steep, narrow and winding Bridge Street and past the Market Cross they pulled the carriage, preceded by the band of

Colonel Hughes' Royal Carmarthenshire Fusiliers. Outside the White Lion Inn in Queen Street, Sir Thomas Picton stood up in his carriage, stilled the commotion around him with a wave of his hand, and gruffly thanked all for what he described as a "handsome and unlooked for compliment" before announcing to the great delight of all that that compliment would be returned, with "a plentiful supply of ale". And in its time-honoured way, the town that had taken Picton to its heart celebrated his return until the small hours of the morning.

And then he went home. To Iscoed, the red-brick mansion overlooking the river, down near the Ferryside, to recover from wounds and illness sustained in his country's service, while the war continued to its inevitable outcome.

Carmarthen learned of Napoleon's defeat, abdication and exile to Elba eighteen months later, in the second week of April, 1814, when:

> The great and glorious news of the downfall of the ferocious tyrant and desolator of Europe was received in this town with the most enthusiastic joy. The bells continued ringing two whole days, and on Tuesday night [the 15th of April] a general and unusually brilliant illumination took place. The town was one blaze of light, the most striking object on this occasion being Furnace House, the residence of Doctor Morgan. The windows displayed wreaths of flowers with laurel and other emblematical leaves tastefully entwined, and the very extensive iron railings at the front were completely covered with lights. The following inscription in the window of the Rev. Mr. Cole produced considerable attraction: 'By the finger of God and in the valour of the allies, the haughtiness of man is laid low.'
>
> The Mayor, attended by several of the Corporation and preceded by a band of music playing 'The Fall of Paris', went in procession through the principal streets of the town and afterwards treated the persons in their suite with a plentiful supply of ale.
>
> Notwithstanding that squibs, crackers, rockets and pistols innumerable were set off in every direction, we are happy to say that no serious accident occurred on this occasion.

And so it was over. Or so it seemed in the months before Napoleon's escape from Elba and his march to Waterloo.

For Europe, 1815 meant the return and final eclipse of Napoleon. For the people of Carmarthen it meant the departure of their hero, Lieutenant General Sir Thomas

Iscoed, Picton's home near the Ferryside.

Furnace House (now the Carmarthen Library), where Picton dined with the Mayor before leaving to join Wellington's army in Belgium.

Picton, for another campaign. His journey to that campaign began by chaise from Iscoed and by the London coach from the Ivy Bush Inn three weeks before the fateful battle of Waterloo. In a prophetic toast which he raised at dinner in Furnace House[3] the night before his departure, the fifty-seven years old veteran drank to "A Coronet, or Westminster Abbey"—or, as others have put it, "Death or Glory."

On the 26th of May, 1815, it was reported that:

> Our gallant countryman, General Sir Thomas Picton, takes his departure this day for the Headquarters of the United British and

> Belgian Army, under the command of the Duke of Wellington, and we most sincerely wish him fresh opportunities for the display of those consummate talents to which his distinguished achievements have borne such frequent testimony.

Two weeks later, on the 16th June:

> Lieutenant General Sir Thomas Picton had the honour of being presented to His Royal Highness the Prince Regent [the future King George IV] at the levee at Carlton House, on his appointment to the Staff in Flanders. On Monday night [the 12th of June] that gallant officer, with his Aide-de-Camp &c. embarked at Ramsgate for Ostend, where in all probability as the wind has been fair, they landed on the following day.

It is difficult in the age of television and instant communication to imagine the rumour and speculation which substituted for news at a time when it could take weeks for news of an event on the Continent to reach the more remote parts of Britain, but the bringing to Carmarthen of news of Waterloo affords a prime example. Five days after this monumental and decisive battle fought on Sunday 18th of June 1815, which had left forty-five thousand men and ten thousand horses dead and dying, heaped on a field no wider than the distance from Carmarthen's Priory Street to Picton's monument at the other end of town, the *Carmarthen Journal* reflected the confused state of the reporting from the battlefield:

> Among a thousand rumours that prevailed this morning it was said that the French General Grenier and his staff had come over to the allies, that Ney had been killed, and Bertrand and Vandamme taken prisoner.
>
> As we anticipated, our illustrious countryman, Sir Thomas Picton, has covered himself with glory. It is stated on the authority of accounts received at Margate by the 'Prince of Wales' packet boat that General Picton's division had neither artillery nor cavalry to sustain the incessant attacks of the enemy. Lord Hay and Colonel Cameron it is stated are among the killed, and General Picton among the wounded. We trust that this account will not prove correct.

The account was indeed incorrect, and tragically so, for Picton had died at Waterloo with a French bullet in his brain. To the end he was the brave eccentric, arriving at Quatre Bras (the action preceding Waterloo) dressed in a shabby old civilian greatcoat and a battered old top hat, having lost his uniform in his rush from England to the battlefield. His ribs broken by a musket ball and in severe pain, he had concealed the fact for fear of being invalided before the main battle, which was clearly imminent.

As at Badajoz, so at Waterloo. Picton's personal courage and decisive action on the field of battle helped to save the day. The division which he led forward in two ranks into the gap left by the wholesale retreat of the Belgian Brigade at a critical stage of the battle, formed the only infantry between the French and Brussels. Seeing the Belgians break and run, the French infantry had deployed for the pursuit and the breakthrough, to be met by Picton and a line of scarlet rising from the reverse slope. The French were stopped in their tracks by a volley from three thousand muskets at forty paces, and the crash of that volley was followed by Picton's shout—"Charge, Hurrah, Hurrah" . . . his last words.

At that instant he was shot through the temple, falling on the neck of his horse as his troops ran at the French and engaged them in a furious bayonet fight which shattered their ranks. The cavalry charge which completed that phase of the battle is legendary, and though such sentiments are no longer fashionable, one cannot imagine that Sir Thomas Picton would have wished to die in any other way, or in any other company.

The people of Carmarthen were stunned when the news reached them twelve days later, on the 30th of June, and the town was in deep mourning as their hero's body was landed in Kent and taken to his London residence. The old soldier was laid to rest on Monday the 3rd of July, 1815, in the Picton family vault in the burial ground of Saint George's, Hanover Square, in London,[4] in the presence of a galaxy of distinguished soldier-mourners and of his brother Edward. His popularity nationally was reflected in the presence of a "great concourse of people assembled to witness the impressive scene", many of whom read the inscription on the coffin plate:

> Lieutenant General Sir Thomas Picton, aged 57, who at the great and decisive battle fought at Waterloo, Flanders, on the 18th June, 1815, between the French Army commanded by Napoleon Buonaparte himself, and the British Army commanded by His

**Picton's body is carried from the field (bottom left) as the Duke of Wellington** orders Lord Uxbridge to launch the cavalry charge. *(National Army Museum).*

> Grace the Duke of Wellington, fell gloriously, according to the words of the Gazette account and in the words of the illustrious Chief—'Leading his Division to the charge with bayonets, by which one of the most serious attacks made by the enemy on our positions was defeated'.

At the same moment, over two hundred miles away, Carmarthen was paying its own tribute. By order of the Mayor, Doctor Charles Morgan, Picton's host at dinner on the night before his departure to join Wellington's army, the bells of Saint Peter's Church rang muffled in "a mournful ceremony" which was continued until well into the night.

Carmarthen honoured its hero in July, 1828, when its Chief Constable, James Evans, "Bright-smith and zinc worker", mustered his twelve town constables for a rare full turnout,[5] on the occasion of the dedication of the first monument to Sir Thomas Picton. It was not often that the constables were seen in such a body, and this occasion eminently suited the ceremonial and nominal nature of their office, providing an opportunity for them to don their gold-embroidered tricorn hats and long cloaks, and to sport their emblazoned staves of office.

At half past eleven in the morning of Tuesday the 28th of July, 1828, they assembled in the Guildhall with:

. . . members of the Corporation, subscribers to the monument &c. who were to go in procession to assist at the ceremony or to be spectators of it.

When all the necessary arrangements were made, the procession moved from the hall in the following order: Town Crier; Chief Constable; 12 Constables; 7 stand of Colours borne by natives of the town; 6 silk banners having inscribed on them in large characters some of the principal battles in which the gallant Picton had been engaged, viz. Badajoz, Ciudad Rodrigo, Vittoria, Pyrennees, Ortez, Toulouse, Le Quatre Bras, Waterloo; 60 Waterloo Veterans, each wearing a sprig of laurel in his hat; Military Band of Music; Staff of the Carmarthen Militia under the command of Captain Harding, in full regimentals and under arms; Corporation of Carmarthen; Subscribers to the monument, &c. &c.

To the strains of martial music, the Town Crier, the Chief Constable and his men led the long and colourful procession through the crowded square, up Lammas Street and away up the Johnstown road, to where the Grecian column, topped by Picton's statue, dominated the skyline. A huge crowd spread across the surrounding fields as the troops and standard bearers took up their positions facing the base of the column, drawing inspiration from the vivid battlefield scenes depicted on its frieze. What memories crowded upon those sixty Waterloo veterans as they gazed on the frieze and the battle-honour scrolls; what "loud and long-continued cheering" arose from them and from the vast concourse as the Honourable George Rice Trevor, M.P., spoke in rousing terms of the man and the times they were honouring and as the air rang with the volleys fired by the red-coated militia, while across the fields from the river there came the roll of cannon as flag-bedecked sailing ships gave their own salute of nineteen guns. And then, with the echoes of 'God Save the King' ringing in their ears, the procession, led again by James Evans and his crimson-clad constables, marched back to the Guildhall Square to be regaled with a stirring speech from John Jones of Ystrad, Johnstown, Member of Parliament for the Borough of Carmarthen.[6] And then:

About a hundred gentlemen sat down to an excellent lunch at the Ivy Bush. The Hon. Rice Trevor, M.P. [for the County] in the chair and John Jones, Esquire, [for the Borough] beside him.

The first Picton Monument: 1827 to 1846. *(Carmarthen Museum).*

The viands consisted of every delicacy in season in the utmost profusion and the wines were superior. Several excellent speeches were delivered in the course of the repast allusive to the event they had met to commemorate, and everything passed off with undisturbed hilarity.

Among the toasts that were drunk were the following: 'The King', three times three; 'The High Sheriff of the County' and 'The Lord Lieutenant', three times three (and so on to the extent of twenty toasts, all 'three times three'!)

From the Ivy Bush, the company walked in the afternoon sunshine along King Street, through Guildhall Square and down Quay Street to the riverside to see the boat races, which:

. . . drew together an immense assemblage. The weather was delightfully serene and the river was covered with boats plying in various directions, while the banks were lined with thousands of spectators, a very considerable proportion of whom were elegantly dressed females.

All the shipping in the river was covered with people, even to the cross-trees,[7] where they hung in clusters and enjoyed a bird's eye view of the whole river.

Upon a given signal, four boats of the first class took their station, viz. John Jones M.P.'s cutter, Hugh Williams Esquire's wherry, a gig from Llanelli and another from Tenby. Upon the discharge of a gun from one of the vessels, the whole started in beautiful style, animated by the cheers of the immense concourse assembled. It was soon evident that Mr. Jones' cutter would come in first, for she shot ahead of her opponents before they proceeded a hundred yards, and then continued to maintain her superiority to the end of the race.

Among the many other events was:

. . . the coracle race, which was well contested and excited much mirth. Ten coracles started and it was surprising to see the dexterity with which the men managed the paddles and impelled their skin-clad skiffs.[8]

The whole of the amusements were plentifully spiced with cheering and firing, both indispensable to give aquatic sports éclat.

The day ended with a grand ball at the Boar's Head Inn which was 'numerously and fashionably attended', while outside, crowds of drinking, singing revellers packed streets aglow with blazing tar barrels and alive with crackling

The second Picton Monument, in 1861. *(National Library of Wales).*

fireworks and the reports of pistols and shotguns. Carmarthen was celebrating in its own inimitable style!

Dawn broke on an exhausted town. The tired but happy dancers emerged blinking into the bright morning sunlight from the Boar's Head, as waiting carriages moved in line to its entrance. Clattering away down Lammas Street, the livery of their coachmen and the finery of their passengers contrasted sharply with the ragged garb of the scavengers and labourers now emerging from their cottages to begin another day's work.

As to the monument which had been the centre-piece of that day of celebration, its ornate beauty proved to be only skin deep. It had been constructed of inferior stone and within eighteen years it crumbled into ruin. So dilapidated was Picton's monument by September, 1846, that this sarcastic comment appeared in the *Carmarthen Journal:*

> A stranger passing by this melancholy looking affair on the Pembroke Mail Coach exclaimed 'Well, I never saw a lime-kiln in the middle of a turnpike road before.' It was not a bad guess, for it looks more like that than anything else. The monument truly is like a man's character—it is easier to pull it to pieces than to set it right again!

In the event, no attempt was made to "set it right again" and a simple obelisk was raised on the same site, from where it still dominates the western approach to the town. The rubble from the old monument was dispersed, but about a hundred and thirty years afterwards a man clearing undergrowth from the back wall of his garden in Johnstown discovered a large piece of carved stone serving as part of his wall. It was part of the frieze, and that solitary remnant on which those sixty Waterloo veterans gazed all those years ago now has a more dignified resting place . . . the Carmarthen Museum, in the carefully restored Bishop's Palace at Abergwili, just outside the town.

And to-day, over a century and a half since the town's hero died on the field of battle, let the visitor to Carmarthen's Guildhall gaze upon the portrait of Picton in the court-room; let him look at the commanding figure and blazing Badajoz behind it, and if he would know the man he sees, let him ponder these words:

> In private life Picton was warm in his friendship, but strong in his enmities. He had a very strict sense of honour, which would not brook the petty deceptions of society. His manners were brusque and his speech blunt and without respect of persons.
>
> As a soldier he was a stern disciplinarian, cold in manner, calm in judgement, yet when excited overwhelmed with passion. He had the foresight of a born commander, possessing considerable power of combination, strong nerve and undaunted courage.[9]

NOTES

[1] See *A Shilling for Carmarthen,* for his experiences and the violence to which he was subjected by the mob during the Reform election riots of 1831.

[2] *The Great Duke,* Sir Arthur Bryant, C.H. (Collins & Sons, London, 1971).

[3] The home of Doctor Charles Morgan, the Mayor, now the Carmarthen Public Library.

[4] Sir Thomas Picton's body was removed to Saint Paul's Cathedral in 1859, to join that of his old chief, the Duke of Wellington, who was buried there in November, 1852.

[5] Only three or four of these were "active" constables. For the rest it was an honorary title, bestowed on them by the party in power in acknowledgement of their support and their votes.

[6] John Jones (1777—1842) lived in a house called Ystrad, in the village named after him—Johnstown—at the western end of Carmarthen. He represented the Borough in Parliament and his experiences in the turbulent 'Reform' elections are recounted in *A Shilling for Carmarthen.*

Lieut. General Sir Thomas Picton, with Badajoz blazing in the background. *(National Army Museum)*.

[7] High in the ships' rigging, at the points where upper masts are joined to lower.
[8] This was one side of the coraclemen of Carmarthen. A rather more lively side is depicted in *A Shilling for Carmarthen,* particularly in Chapter 8—'The Ebbing Tide'.
[9] *The Dictionary of National Biography,* 1895.

## Sergeant John Samuel
## Waterloo Medal

'Full Military Honours' meant exactly that at a Carmarthen soldier's funeral. Military bands, muffled drums, scarlet and blue uniforms, firing parties, regimental colours and long corteges of shiny black carriages pulled by shiny black, plume-nodding horses, followed by huge crowds in all the trappings of mourning. For these were the days of 'Military Glory' and though many of those who had served their country in all parts of the Empire ended their days in the workhouse on Penlan, Military Honours were given whenever the army and the townspeople became aware of their demise, and they were given in Carmarthen in full measure.

A military funeral of great proportions was afforded Carmarthen's last surviving Peninsular and Waterloo veteran, a comrade-in-arms, so to speak, of the town's great hero, Thomas Picton. On Tuesday the 20th of October, 1874—almost sixty years after Waterloo—ex-sergeant John Samuels was buried, at the age of eighty-eight years. The huge funeral procession moved away from his home in Waun Dew (Richmond Terrace) under Militia standards, to the beat of muffled drums and to the solemn lamentations of a funeral march. Led by Chief Constable Brown-Edwardes, late Captain of the Carmarthen Militia, in sword-girded full-dress uniform, the cortege moved slowly through Dark Gate and up Lammas Street to Saint David's Church. An obituary in the *Carmarthen Journal* told of Sergeant Samuels' military exploits:

> John Samuel entered the service in the year 1807 (sixty-seven years before his death) by enlistment in the Carmarthen Fusiliers, and in 1811 he enlisted into the 1st Royals. He was soon sent to the Peninsula and took part in the Battles of Salamanca and Vittoria.[1] He was wounded in the breast during the siege of San Sebastian. He served also in the West Indies. He arrived from

Jamaica in time to join the Duke of Wellington's army at Brussels and to go into action at Waterloo. He was one of the letter orderlies and was wounded early in the fight, in the knee. In his disabled state he contrived to crawl to the church yard at Waterloo and succeeded in staunching his wound and remained there overnight. The day after the battle he was conveyed to Brussels, where he soon recovered.

He was discharged from the service on the 8th of October, 1833, with a Sergeant's pension. While in the army he was regarded as a good and efficient soldier and maintained the same character for sobriety and integrity up to the day of his death. The old soldier had been a communicant in Saint David's Church for the last thirty years.

Rifles rattled Carmarthen's last farwell over the grave on that October morning in 1874 . . . the last farewell to a soldier from a vanished age.

NOTES

[1] Sir Thomas Picton was at both battles, but at Salamanca he was too ill to take part.

## The Sepoy General

On Wednesday the 11th of September, 1844, Major General Sir William Nott, G.C.B., returned to his home town, Carmarthen, after forty four years in India.

Born in Neath in 1782, William Nott came to Carmarthen at the age of twelve, when his father became landlord of the Ivy Bush coaching inn—the same landlord who welcomed Lord Nelson and Lady Hamilton on their stay at that establishment. A spell in the Carmarthen Volunteers gave the young William a taste for soldiering and in 1800, at the age of eighteen, he sailed away to India, to a commission in Bengal with the army of the Honourable East India Company.

Following in the steps of Clive of India, the company's most famous servant, William Nott gained a brilliant reputation as a commander in the field and as an administrator, in both of which capacities he developed a deep understanding of the people and their native rulers. He it was who played a leading part in salvaging his country's military reputation from the disasters brought about by bungling politicians and inept Queen's (as opposed to company's) generals, all of whom came under the lash of Nott's contempt for those who he said had "... bared the throat of every European in this country to the sword and knife of the revengeful Afghan and the bloody Belooch".

The massacre of sixteen thousand British and Indian troops, wives, children and camp followers in the narrow passes of the North West Frontier during their retreat from the Afghanistan capital of Kabul in 1842 was the most appalling disaster ever to befall a British Army . . . and it had to be avenged. The task fell to the 'Company' generals—the 'Sepoy' generals—and it was carried out in a brilliant series of victories culminating in the capture of Kabul by an army that had marched there through the rocky passes from India, over the bleached bones of its comrades—an army that now exacted vengeance in full measure.

William Nott—that "capable officer of rather irritable temperament", that "man of some talents but blunt address", that "honest, plain-spoken soldier, not always right, but always believing himself to be right; hearty, genuine and sincere"[2]—became a national hero. He was invested with the G.C.B. (as Knight Grand Cross of the Order of the Bath) and when in February, 1843, both Houses of Parliament voted their thanks to the victorious generals, the seventy-four year old Duke of Wellington—Picton's old chief—honoured William Nott by singling him out as the best of them. And Sir Robert Peel said of Nott that:

> During the whole of the time he was employed in these dangerous undertakings, his gallant spirit never forsook him, and he dreamt of nothing but vindicating his country's honour.

And now, at the age of sixty-three, he was coming home. In an age when war and military achievement still had the aura of glory, a soldier here was a hero indeed, and for the people of Carmarthen there had been no one like Sir William Nott since Picton's time, thirty years before. Placards all over the town announced his coming and the 11th of September, 1844, saw the:

Major General Sir William Nott, wearing the insignia of the GCB and his Afghan Medal. *(Carmarthen Museum).*

Triumphal entry of Major General Sir William Nott, G.C.B., to Carmarthen: It having been notified to the Mayor of Carmarthen that Sir William Nott would enter this town on Wednesday at one o'clock from Kidwelly, at which place he slept the previous night, every preparation was made to receive him with due honour.

The morning was ushered in by the ringing of bells at Saint Peter's Church, and the streets gradually filled with people from the surrounding country. The Guildhall and its environs were filled by the most respectable persons of the town, the streets were crowded and all was joyous bustle. Each street had its festoons hung across it, composed of garlands of flowers, ribbons and boughs of trees.

About a quarter past twelve o'clock the procession left the hall under the able direction of Mr. George Goode, preceded by the Societies of Oddfellows and True Ivorites, decked out with showy scarves and knots of ribbons and flowers, with their curious and splendid insignia, which contributed much to the show, and accompanied by bands of music and numerous banners. They were followed by the Mayor and Aldermen in their scarlet gowns, the Recorder and the Town Council. Then came the gentlemen of the town and neighbourhood, four abreast, and thus the procession proceeded to about three quarters of a mile out of the town, when a halt was called.

The Pensarn Turnpike Gate was very pretilly ornamented with a pendant wreath and festoons of boughs of trees and flowers. Soon afterwards the Swansea Mail came up and brought the news that the General would arrive in about half an hour.

In rather less than that time the Hero came, and was greeted with loud and joyous acclamations. His horses were immediately taken out, ropes were attached to his carriage and a number of sturdy fellows were put ready to draw it into the town.

But the assembled thousands had a shock, for:

Sir William, who was in plain clothes, but with a military undress cap on his head looked fatigued and ill, and scarcely able to bear the excitement of the scene.

The following address, prepared for the occasion, was here read to him:

'The Major General Sir William Nott, G.C.B. We, the Mayor, Recorder and Corporation and inhabitants of Carmarthen, beg to offer you our warmest congratulations on your arrival in your native country and our ardent wishes for the speedy restoration of your health. We have witnessed with pride and gratification the splendid achievements which have obtained for you the highest military distinction it is in the power of your Sovereign to bestow, the thanks of both Houses of Parliament and the admiration and gratitude of your country.

We pray that a gracious providence will long preserve your valuable life to enable you to enjoy the honours so nobly won by your consummate skill and undaunted bravery and which has shed a brilliant lustre on the country of your birth and established your distinguished military fame. William Morris, Mayor.'

The veteran was so overcome that his reply was scarcely audible. The tears gushed from his eyes as he told the Mayor 'He could have faced an army of his country's foes with much less emotion than he could his native townsmen's kindness, but that he would soon have another opportunity of thanking them with more calmness.'

Several bystanders cried 'Enough, Enough. Sit down General', and an affecting incident here took place. A Sergeant of the 41st Foot, which Regiment was at Kandahar with him, stepped up to the carriage and said 'Welcome home, General.' The veteran gazed at him a few seconds, saw the Afghan ribbon in his button hole and then said 'Give me your hand', and the General and the Private soldier grasped each other's hands as friends. It may be questioned if this simple welcome did not thrill to the heart of his old commander even more than the general acclaim of the assembled thousands.

The procession, as ncarly as could be guessed about a quarter of a mile in length, now retraced its steps. The General, who was accompanied by his wife and daughters, followed immediately after the Corporate Body. And so, with the booming of cannon from the Old Castle Green, the cheering of the multitude and the waving of handkerchiefs from crowded windows, the old soldier paraded through Carmarthen.

Guildhall Square and Lammas Street had a most animating appearance when the General stood up and turned from side to side—observing and observed of all. Truly it was a glorious hour for the Hero.

When he arrived at his brother's residence in Picton Terrace, he lingered on the steps of the carriage as though desirous of addressing the multitude, but it would not do as he was quite overpowered, and he was assisted from his carriage and up the steps to the house by the Mayor and the Recorder. The General's age appears to be about sixty-five, and his head is perfectly white and his countenance is not unlike that of the Duke of Wellington, having an aquiline nose.

Many of his companions in arms caught his eye in his passage through the streets and had signs of recognition. One of them observed to a comrade 'He looks very natural, don't he?' An old woman in Lammas Street was waving a large flag from a window, which it required her utmost strength to do. The General, observing her, smiled and nodded, and the old lady curtsied again and again in evident confusion.

It had been arranged to give a grand dinner in commemoration of the arrival of the Carmarthen Hero, but it is entirely dependent upon his health, which at present appears to be in a bad state, although it may be held that the appearance is worse than the reality in consequence of the overpowering excitement of the day.

The townspeople's hopes that the General's fatigue might be a temporary reaction to his strenuous journey and his tremendous reception were dashed; within three months, without emerging again from his brother's house, the old soldier was dead. In the first week of January, in accordance with a wish he had expressed as he lay dying, his body 'Lay in State', and:

> . . . for several days, numbers availed themselves of the melancholy privilege. Arrangements for exhibiting the remains of the deceased were of the simplest kind, attended by no other 'State' than what association and his imperishable military fame invested in him.

On Tuesday the 7th of January, 1845, a grey, bleak winter's day, the coffin was followed through the town, from Picton Terrace, down Lammas Street, through Guildhall Square and King Street, to Saint Peter's Church, by a huge crowd, silently walking behind the Mayor, the Corporation and many carriages—every man and woman there wearing black scarves and hatbands—to the accompaniment of Saint Peter's muffled bells. And the Hero was laid to rest, alongside his father and mother in the Church yard there.

He is commemorated now by a statue cast from the bronze of cannon captured at Maharajpur in India, and given for the purpose by the Honourable East India Company. The statue was brought to the town from Bristol by the paddle steamer

Nott's Monument in the 1860s. *(National Library of Wales).*

'Phoenix' and placed in the old heart of the town—the site of the ancient markets, renamed Nott Square in his honour.

NOTES

[1]Sir John Kaye: 'History of the War in Afghanistan', 1851, quoted in *Signal Catastrophe; The Retreat from Kabul,* Patrick Macrory (Hodder & Stoughton Ltd., 1966).

Sergeant Major Kyle's funeral parade on Monday the 14th of February, 1870, was one of the most impressive ever . . . saving, of course, that of his old General, William Nott. It was a send-off befitting the man whose natural role it had become to organise, drill and marshal all the parades by which Carmarthen delighted in marking great occasions. A big man, with a voice to match, the epitome of the Regimental Sergeant Major, Kyle's regular service with the 41st (Welch) Regiment had been extended to a staff post at the Carmarthen Barracks with the Royal Carmarthenshire Rifle Militia—the local volunteer corps—and he gained an immense popularity among the people of the town. His military record was equally impressive:

> The Gallant Veteran entered the army when only 16 years of age and served with the 41st Regiment all through the campaign commanded by the late General Nott when the latter by Herculean exertions retrieved the military character of his nation in Central Asia by repelling the Afghans to recapture Kandahar in 1842. Mr. Kyle also served with the army in the Punjab and received several medals for his brilliant and meritorious services in India from Private to Sergeant Major, extending over a period of eighteen years. After completing his term of service he retired as Sergeant Major of his Regiment on a well-earned pension and was appointed to the same position in the Royal Carmarthenshire Militia about thirteen years ago, then under the command of the late Colonel Lord Dynevor.
>
> His stentorian voice and steady martial bearing at drill in the old time will never be forgotten and it was one of the proudest moments of his life when he received through his Captain, Brown-Edwardes[1] the congratulations of General Hutchinson that the Carmarthenshire Rifle Volunteers of a hundred strong was the best drilled corps in the 8,000 volunteers who attended the memorable review at Gloucester in 1862.

The sombre rhythm of funeral marches emanating from the band of a hundred musicians smothered the town as the 2nd Battalion of the Volunteers rested on their arms reversed and the firing party raised their rifles and fired their last salute over their old R.S.M.'s grave, and the day ended on a cold, grey and drizzly note as the many hundreds of mourners left the

Sergeant Major John Kyle, in the uniform of the Royal Carmarthenshire Rifle Militia. *(Carmarthen Museum).*

**Capt. Brown-Edwardes of Rhydygors, who, as Chief Constable of Carmarthen**, led Sgt. Major Kyle's funeral procession. (Seen here in the uniform of the Royal Carmarthenshire Rifle Militia, in the centre of the picture). *(Carmarthen Museum).*

cemetery. But the pubs of the town were warm and aglow with nostalgia as old soldiers smoked pipes of tobacco and drank gallons of ale over recollections of campaigns on the North West Frontier of India and of battles on the Alma Heights, at Balaclava and Inkerman, of hand-to-hand fighting for the strongholds of Sebastopol, and of punitive expeditions and peace-keeping operations in all the far-flung outposts of the Queen's Empire.

As has been said of the object of many a similar funeral . . . old Kyle would have enjoyed it all!

NOTE

[1]Captain Brown-Edwardes was Chief Constable of the Carmarthen Borough Police Force (*The Carmarthen Shilling*) from 1871 to 1875.

The end of the Crimean war came as something of an anti-climax to the people of Carmarthen, who felt—like the rest of the British people—that their army was being robbed of the opportunity to teach the Russians a thorough lesson. After all, this was a war that had been virtually forced on a wavering government by the clamour of the public and the popular press because of a fancied threat to Britain's Imperial pretensions in the eastern Mediterranean. A thorough shambles from beginning to end, with blunders ranging from the scandalous waste of life brought about by the neglect of medical and supply services, to inconclusive and dearly-bought victories,[1] and to the fiasco of the charge of the Light Brigade, this war needed a clear-cut grand finale to assuage the people's anger and hide their shame . . . and there wasn't one.[2] No wonder that when the news reached Carmarthen by the new electric telegraph on Monday morning the 31st of March, 1856:

> . . . though the merry peals of the excellent set of bells belonging to the venerable fabric of Saint Peter's continued almost without intermission throughout the day, in fact most of the inhabitants seemed to think that the peace was a 'mockery, an illusion and a snare', the popular idea being that now the English[*sic*] have 'got their coats off and are ready for work' they ought to be allowed to go in and win thc fight.

And the reluctance of the townspeople showed through even when Queen Victoria commanded a general holiday and celebrations to greet the Peace. Although celebratory processions were something of a Carmarthen speciality, this one earned nothing but derision:

> A 'Procession' (heaven defend us from such a procession again) indulged the town by displaying its proportions in the morning. Its component parts were six or eight flags with a similar number of flag-bearers, the Hallkeeper in his sprucest costume, and the immortal and ever-to-be-remembered 'Town Band', which 'discoursed' most abominable 'music' (if that be not a profanation of the term) throughout the entire morning and to the horror of Her Majesty's disgusted subjects. The 'Procession' was most appropriately headed by an idiot.

No such reluctance dampened the welcome given to the

returning heroes, though, especially that of Henry Lawrence, doctor, magistrate's son, veteran of the battles of Alma and Inkerman, and of the siege of Sebastopol:

> The Bells of Old Saint Peter's Church rang out their merriest welcome on Tuesday morning (the 15th of July, 1856) in honour of the return to his home of Henry Lawrence, M.D., Premier Assistant Surgeon to the Grenadier Guards, who has been out with his Regiment in the Crimea throughout the whole of the Russian War. We are happy to add that he returned in the most robust health and strength, that he accompanied the Guards on their triumphant entry into London and that he was received with rapture by all his relatives and old acquaintances.
>
> The Carmarthen Brass Band paraded the town in the evening and serenaded Doctor Lawrence for a lengthy period.

As to the Monument, the townspeople were delighted and touched by the decision of Colonel Lysons and his brother officers of the 23rd Regiment, the Royal Welsh Fusiliers, to place their tribute to their dead comrades in Carmarthen, of all the towns in Wales. In October, 1857, the *Carmarthen Journal* carried a large engraving of the design, complete with its cast-iron railing formed of crossed muskets, and explained that:

> On the shaft and pedestal will be inscribed the names of all the officers, non-commissioned officers and privates who were the victims of the late Russian War, whether killed on the field of battle or cut off by pestilential disease.
>
> It is gratifying in the highest degree to have the Monument erected in this town, as many of our County families have at different periods had some of their members in the 23rd Regiment. We may instance the families of Cwmgwili, Tregib and Rhydygorse, the late Rev. Edward Morris who formerly held a commission in the Corps, and several others.
>
> The design is chaste and elegant and when the erection is complete it will be an ornament not only to this town but also to the principality.

Unlike that of Picton's Monument, its unveiling on the 20th of September, 1858, was a muted affair, in keeping with the fact that many families in the town had been bereaved by this wasteful war. It was for the sake of their feelings that none of the customary military show or bonfires or fireworks were included in the ceremony. The large captured Russian cannon

The Fusilier Monument in the 1860s. *(National Library of Wales).*

which was placed in front of the monument was no mere ornament; it served to enliven future celebrations of other events and victories in booming out its salute across the river. Its long barrel served, too, as a receptacle for flaggons of ale, placed there by the landlords of the Coopers Arms, The Harp and other nearby pubs for the refreshment of the policemen on the night beats!

The cannon has gone now, and the monument stands worn and neglected, a symbol of another age, its uniqueness forgotten with the passing years.

## NOTES

[1]Britain's army numbered 27,000 at the outset. 25,000 died, most of them the flower of the army and the remainder raw recruits sent out to replace them. Disease and neglect killed over 18,000 . . . more than had died or been wounded in battle.

[2]The government was swept out of office on a tidal wave of public opinion and press criticism over its mishandling of the prosecution of the war and its appalling neglect of the army.

## PRIVATE DAVID THOMAS
## 4th LIGHT DRAGOONS

Honour the Light Brigade. A record of the services of Officers, Non-Commissioned Officers and men of the five Light Cavalry Regiments which made up the Light Brigade at Balaclava on October 25th, 1854 and saw service in the Crimea from September 1854 to the end of the War:

1118 THOMAS (PRIVATE DAVID)
Enlisted: 1843.
Rode in the Charge: 25th October, 1854.
Medals: Crimea, Distinguished Conduct Medal.
Member, Balaclava Commemoration Society, 1879.[1]

There was an awful note of sadness about the circumstances surrounding Carmarthen's farwell to its last "Balaclava hero". David Thomas lived in Little Water Street and in 1843, at the age of twenty-one, he joined the 4th Light Dragoons, who were stationed in Carmarthen's Penlan Workhouse in the aftermath of their spectacular charge into the mob besieging the workhouse during the Rebecca Riots.[2] Eleven years later he and his Regiment arrived in the Crimea with the Light Brigade of Cavalry under the Earl of Cardigan.

Like his comrades, David Thomas sat astride his horse watching the assault by the infantry on the Alma Heights, frustrated and furious that the cavalry were obliged to be mere spectators. He joined in the half-hearted pursuit of the fleeing Russians and he endured all the boredom and fatigue of camp duty, stand-to and patrol that were the lot of the cavalry until there came the moment he and his comrades had been hoping for and feared would never come: the moment when Lord Cardigan's strong hoarse voice, cutting across a deathly silence broken only by the clink of harness and spurs, the swish of

The 4th Light Dragoons in the Crimea. *(National Army Museum).*

swords drawn from scabbards and the flutter of lance pennants, shouted his fateful order—"The Brigade will advance! First Squadron of the 17th Lancers direct!" And David Thomas, thinking never to see old Carmarthen again, pointed his sabre to the front and charged with the rest through the cross-fire, down the valley of death, into the smoke and flame of the Russian guns.

David Thomas's survival, like that of the other 190 or so survivors of the 700 who charged with the Light Brigade was nothing short of a miracle, but, large, powerful man that he was, he not only cut his way through the Russian gunners, but picked up one of his badly wounded officers and brought him back to the British lines. That officer never forgot David Thomas for as long as he lived and for years sent money to him in his retirement back in Carmarthen. When the officer died, David Thomas was left with "the pittance of ninepence [less than 4p] a day which a grateful country presented him in recognition of his valorous service",[3] and was eventually forced to seek refuge in the Penlan Workhouse, where he died on the 20th of March, 1890, at the age of sixty-eight, and thirty six years after the Charge of the Light Brigade.

The Light Brigade cuts its way through the Russian gunners. Here, Private David Thomas saved the life of one of his officers. *(National Army Museum).*

Life had turned full circle, for David Thomas ended his days in the very building in which he had first taken the Queen's Shilling to become a cavalryman in Her Majesty's 4th Light Dragoons. It was only then that Carmarthen woke up to the fact that it had lost a link with history, and all the stops were pulled out:

> On Monday afternoon, the remains of David Thomas, the Carmarthen Balaclava Hero, were interred at the Carmarthen Cemetery with Military Honours. The solemn and impressive cortege started from the residence of the deceased at 36 Little Water Street at four o'clock and wended its way through the main thoroughfares of the town, to reach the cemetery at five-fifteen.
>
> The order of procession was as follows: Firing party of twelve members of the 1st Volunteer Battalion, Welch Regiment, in charge of Colour Sergeant Lewis and headed by Corporal Williams in full dress; Band of the Corps, amalgamated with the bandsmen of the Carmarthenshire Royal Artillery Militia under the conductorhsip of Bandmaster Jones, followed by the open hearse containing the coffin, which was covered with the Union Jack, wreaths and crosses. Then came the mourning carriage with members of the bereaved family; then a company of Volunteers in charge of Sergeant Major Cooper and members of the Royal

Artillery Militia, followed by a large number of influential townspeople, who attended to show their great respect for one who had so faithfully served and defended his country.

The Last Post sounded. The ragged crack of a rifle volley echoed around the valley of Trevaughan and Ffynnondrain. And as the crowds of "influential townspeople" began to break away from the graveside and move towards the cemetery gates, a collection was taken among them towards the cost of the funeral expenses. The amount realised fell six shillings [30p] short of the amount needed—a deficiency made good by a reluctant relative!

The pubs of Carmarthen were, as always, full in the aftermath of a military funeral. But there were none left to reminisce about the Charge of the Light Brigade, and, unlike Sergeant Major Kyle, David Thomas would probably not have enjoyed his send-off anyway. That deficit of six shillings would probably, as they say, have cast a gloom over the whole proceedings.

## NOTES

[1] *Honour the Light Brigade* (A record of the Services of Officers, Non-Commissioned Officers and Men of the Five Light Cavalry Regiments, which made up the Light Brigade at Balaclava on October 25th, 1854 and saw service in the Crimea from September 1854 to the end of the War), Canon William Murrell Lummis, MC, (J. B. Hayward and son, London, 1973).

[2] See *A Shilling for Carmnarthen,* Chapter 5—BECA—for an account of the invasion of Carmarthen and the attack on the Workhouse.

[3] Carmarthen Journal.

# Soldiers of The Queen

One could always find a policeman at the corner of Dark Gate, below Carmarthen's Guildhall, and Police Constable Number 1 David Jones of the Carmarthen Borough Police[1] was standing there early in the evening of Thursday the 1st of February, 1900, when a breathless Sergeant of the Volunteers paused in his rush down Lammas Street to share the news that had just arrived by telegram at the barracks, news that must be passed to His Worship the Mayor without delay, if P.C. Jones could tell him where he might be found. P.C. Jones could, and did, and there was something of a stir in Saint Mary's Auction Rooms in the narrow street up the side of the Guildhall as the soldier entered. He whispered to an usher, who in turn tiptoed to the stage and whispered to Mayor Walter Spurrell, Chairman of the well-attended musical evening being held there to raise funds for the provision of comforts for the troops fighting the Boers in South Africa.

The audience was applauding a spirited rendering by Mr. Harry Evans of that most popular of patriotic songs 'Who carries the gun?' as the Mayor rose and called forward Colour Sergeant Poole, the epitome of the Victorian soldier—ramrod backed, scarlet tunic crossed by the broad red sash of his rank, pill-box hat at the correct rakish angle, moustache waxed tightly to its pointed ends, and silver-topped 'swagger cane' tucked under his left arm. "Ladies and Gentlemen," said the Mayor, "this is a proud moment for Carmarthen. Colour Sergeant Instructor Poole has just informed me that the commanding officer of our Volunteer Corps has just received a telegram from the War Office in London to say that our ancient borough has been honoured by the selection of three of its Volunteers to join the Welch Regiment at the front in South Africa. They join a troop train at the junction at 2.30 tomorrow." The rest of his words were drowned in cheers and it was several minutes later—after the audience had sung 'Soldiers of the Queen', the 'National Anthem' and 'Mae Hen Wlad Fy Nhadau'—that he was able to announce the names of the lucky three: Johnny Phillips, twenty year old son of John Phillips of the Quay, and a printer with the *Carmarthen Journal;* Theo Rogers,[2] twenty year old son of Lammas Street plumber, David Rogers; James Meredith Williams, twenty-two year old solicitor's clerk, son of John Williams, the Nott Square watchmaker—three of those who had fired their rifles in the *feu de joie* in front of the Guildhall in celebration of their Queen's Diamond Jubilee nearly three years before. And now they were off to share in the glory of fighting her colonial wars.

But those Carmarthen men were to discover what soldiers throughout history have discovered—the difference between the glory of war and the stark reality of the battlefield, a reality that for the first time (at least so far as Carmarthen was

The first Carmarthen volunteers for the Boer War: Sgt. H. C. Langman (rear), Pte. John Phillips, Lance Cpl. James Meredith Williams and Pte. Theo Rogers (left to right). *(Theo Rogers).*

concerned) could be communicated to the people at home. Their letters from embarkation depot, troopship, line of march and battlefield would be reproduced in the local newspapers for the benefit of an expanding readership. The scale of that expansion can be judged by the fact that in 1810 the circulation of the Carmarthen Journal could be counted in three figures. Illiteracy apart, there was a stiff duty on newspapers, designed to keep them out of the hands of the masses for fear of encouraging dissent. In 1900, the Carmarthen Journal printed some 5,000 copies weekly.

There were other Carmarthen men—regular soldiers—in the Regiments fighting in South Africa, but Johnny Phillips, James Meredith Williams and Theo Rogers were the first Saint Peter's Boys to answer the call for volunteers when, as so often, Britain's unpreparedness for war led her standing army into a series of humiliating defeats by an under-rated enemy, in the Autumn of 1899. Mournful Monday, the 29th of October, 1899, had seen the surrender to the Boer farmers of nearly a thousand British troops outside Ladysmith in an engagement which preceded the bottling up of 12,000 more in the town, in a siege that was to last for four months. Mafeking was already surrounded—and would be for the next seven months—by the despised and underestimated Boers, and nearly a thousand troops were bottled up there. But, most humiliating of all, the last year of the century opened with the loss through death, wounds and capture of 1,200 out of 1,700 officers and men in the ill-conceived fiasco of Spion Kop. As in Afghanistan in the 1840s, in the Crimea in the 1850s and in Zululand in the 1870s, the flower of Britain's army was being squandered by stunningly inept generalship.[3]

But this war would have more far-reaching, even earth-shaking, consequences, for in turning the world against the British 'Goliath' and towards the Boer 'David',[4] it convinced the Kaiser that the British were militarily inferior to the Germans, and so sowed some of the seeds of the Great War of 1914-1918.[5] That war, with its three quarters of a million British dead would carry off no less than 3,600 from Carmarthenshire alone, adding yet another war memorial to Carmarthen's unusual collection, which already commemorated Wellington's Peninsular and Waterloo campaigns, the Afghan wars, the Crimean war and the Boer War.

In 1900, though, war could still be 'glorious'. It would take the mud of Flanders' Fields to smother that particular myth. The popular agitation for a declaration of war was tremendous and was as intense in Carmarthen as anywhere else in the Kingdom. But we must not condemn too easily. It requires a great deal of understanding of contemporary ideas and values to get anywhere near to appreciating how such wars could be justified, as they were; how sincerely the people at all levels believed in Britain's Imperial Destiny, and why so many of them fought and worked and died to create and sustain the Empire. It requires that kind of understanding to cope, for example, with such contemporary utterances as:

> The Transvaal Republic had become a centre and rallying point for all that was most bitterly opposed to British supremacy and to the ideals which have made our race so great. So long as we English [*sic*] are faithful to the noblest call of duty and to the highest instincts which are in us as a race, we are helping the cause of progress, which is the cause of God. We know that whatever checks, whatever vicissitudes, whatever disappointments may befall, we march to victory.[6]

Such were the sentiments that justified the despatch to South Africa of 10,000 British and Empire troops to reinforce the 7,000 garrisoned there in the Autumn of 1899, for the purpose of "ending the twenty years' purgatory of misrule in the Transvaal", an independent republic whose integrity had been guaranteed by Britain . . . before the discovery of gold there. And such were the sentiments in the hearts of the people of Carmarthen as they carried young Phillips, Rogers and Williams shoulder high to the troop train at Carmarthen Junction and cheered them on their departure "for the front". They, as would others after them, were answering the call for volunteers to form fresh battalions to support the hard-pressed regulars, who had found all their conceptions of war confounded by an enemy who would not even stand up and fight like a man, but actually fired from cover like a coward!

Trooper D. H. Lewis experienced this at first hand in several bloody engagements. The son of a Carmarthen man (Mr. Edwin Lewis of Greenhall) he served with Thorneycroft's

Mounted Infantry, one of a number of irregular "Colonial" battalions recruited from white Colonial settlers and officered partly by the Colonials themselves and partly by men seconded from regular British cavalry regiments. These mounted infantry brought an unfamiliar dash and mobility to the army in the early days and foreshadowed the style it would be forced to adopt later in the war. Trooper Lewis' commanding officer, burly and fiery Lieutenant Colonel A. W. Thorneycroft, actually found himself in command at one point during the darkness, the confusion and the slaughter of the fight on Spion Kop, when the exposed British were given yet another costly lesson in the consequences of advancing over open ground on an unseen foe. As Trooper Lewis saw that foe:

> They are the biggest funks in creation. You have no idea what immense care they take not to show even the top of a finger tip to an enemy. They absolutely refuse to show a hair over cover, but will take no end of pains to construct holes and breaches so that they may lie completely out of sight.
>
> Even when our fellows are advancing to attack the Boer positions the Boer won't get up, but they actually point the rifle at random in the direction from which we come and pull the trigger without sighting, keeping their bodies meanwhile entirely behind cover!

The cads!

More to his taste was the behaviour of his own side at the battle of Colenso in December, 1899, which—before becoming involved himself and being severely wounded[7]—he watched from rising ground:

> It was a magnificent sight to see the Irish [Infantry] Brigade under General Hart moving towards the enemy. These poor fellows were advancing in quarter column and although the men were mowed down like tall grass before a scythe, the gaps were closed up and all the columns moved on without the slightest appearance of shock or disturbance, just as if they were on parade. I never saw such amazing bravery and coolness in my life. It was marvellous, and heartbreaking.

This was the stuff of Waterloo and Balaclava and though the khaki tunic had replaced the traditional red coat in the field,[8] the British army had not yet learned that the days of the infantry square and the advance in parade-ground order were gone. As an American correspondent in South Africa saw it: "The khaki is the British soldier's only protection. He cannot learn to advance under cover and is sure to stand up and stretch himself against the skyline".[9] The British army would have to suffer the slaughter of the Somme and other futile frontal assaults in the first world war just a few years later before that lesson was finally driven home to its generals.

One of those Generals was Sir Herbert Kitchener, and Carmarthen boy Benjamin Rees, with G Company of the 1st Battalion, The Welch Regiment, was one of those who bore the brunt of just such an act of futility, when Kitchener sent two Divisions in parade-ground order against the hidden Boers at Paardeburg. The Welsh were the first into the attack and were at once pinned down in the open under murderous fire. This was the reality of modern war, which began to be seen by ordinary men now able to articulate their feelings to the folks at home. From Bloemfontein, in April, 1900, Benjamin Rees wrote:

> War is a terrible thing, especially against the Boers, as they are just like us. I have been in two battles—Paardeburg was one where Kronje was captured and about 5,000 prisoners. The battle lasted seven days and you should have seen their laager [camp] after the battle. The dead were piled one on the other, hundreds—yes thousands—of them killed. It made tears roll down my cheeks when I saw it, and many times have I shed a tear when alone thinking of my own comrades who have been killed and wounded.
>
> The second battle lasted one day, at Drieburg, where a hot fire was kept up all day and we lost in the Brigade about 400 killed and wounded. It was a nasty battle, far worse than what I experienced in the first, and thank God for sparing my life.
>
> I have been in the first line in both battles and it is like a Godsend that I was not shot. In my own company alone there are 26 killed and wounded, that is out of a hundred strong. Two of the officers of my company got wounded. One died and the other is not expected to live. We have lost 12 officers and 232 soldiers killed and wounded in our Regiment. You will find there will be a lot of men knocking about with limbs missing after this war is over.
>
> You talk about us living like gentlemen. I could eat all I get in a day as half a meal for breakfast. I am sleeping out in the open air every night since the 10th of February [i.e. for a month] with one blanket, and have had to sleep many a night without one at all,

and raining all night. I have had to go two days without food, such as what they give us.

About the presents sent to us, I have not seen anything but one pound of tobacco from Cardiff, and I think that the whole of the 6th Division, which consists of about 18 to 25,000 men have not seen much more, if so much. Everything has been very badly arranged for the troops out here. You must not believe all the papers publish. I could write all day, but I am tired. I will be very pleased to receive the parcel, if it is only a bun. Give my respects to all, from your affectionate cousin Ben.[10]

It was at about this time that Johnny Phillips, Theo Rogers and James Meredith Williams caught up with their Regiment at the front.

Carmarthen's policemen were out in force early on the day that the three volunteer Saint Peter's Boys were to leave the town. They were out in the knowledge that the townspeople would respond in their customary manner to the Mayor's wish that the young volunteers should have an appropriate send-off:

These young fellows are natives of Carmarthen and, risking their lives as they are doing in this, one of the most momentous crises that the history of the country has ever known, have made themselves representative of some of the best traditions of the old town. They are in the truest sense answering their country's call and in doing so they are running the risk of never returning to their birthplace, and Carmarthen must not allow them to go without acknowledging the honour they reflect upon it.

The deed was as good as the word as the three heroes, resplendent in spiked helmets, scarlet jackets and white pipe-clayed accoutrements, carrying rifles and full kit, reported for duty on the morning of Friday the 2nd of February, 1900:

Throughout the morning the whole town was in a flutter of excitement. The departure of these three Saint Peter's Boys to face the shot and shell of a formidable enemy seemed to give a new meaning to the gravity of the present war. Even the note of the Volunteer bugle sounding the note for the Volunteers to muster for the send-off had an unwonted thrill as the bugler blew his way down King Street.

The Volunteers mustered in strong force at the Armoury at 1.30 p.m. and under the command of Capt. James John and headed by the band of the Corps, marched to the station shortly before 2 o'clock. The three departing men were placed at the front and were immediately hoisted to the shoulders of the crowd. When they emerged into Guildhall Square, the band playing 'Auld Lang Syne', round after round of tremendous cheering rose from the dense crowd which packed the Square and the streets up to Nott's Monument.

The Mayor gave each of them an outfit of underclothing, some money and tobacco from the local War Fund. Tobacco, pipes and pouches were given by Capt. John, while a generous supply of tokens and necessaries were forthcoming from other sources.

And then the procession made its way through King Street, Spilman Street and down Castle Hill. Every window on the line of route was packed with people, who cheered and waved their handkerchiefs in adieu. At the junction station, both platforms were occupied by the crowds till scarcely an inch of space was spare, and the interval before the arrival of the train was whiled away by the whole assemblage singing 'Rule Britannia' and other patriotic airs. As the train steamed into the station cheer after cheer was raised by those on the platform, especially when it was seen that it contained volunteers from down the line. Then, amidst a terrific pushing and cheering, a shouting of farewells, the craning of necks to get the last glimpse of the boys, our men were at last allowed to get into the train, which in a few minutes moved out between the packed crowds who covered the platform and lined the banks at each side of the station.

And that was the last seen of our Redcoats—for a short while only, let us hope.

The feelings of the boys themselves were conveyed back to Carmarthen from their Cardiff billet four days later:

Dear Mr. Mayor: The reason of our writing this letter is to thank the people of Carmarthen for the right royal send-off they gave us on Friday last at so short a notice. It was something to remember as long as we live, and they may rely upon us not to abuse their confidence and to keep untarnished the good name of Saint Peter's Boys. Your loyal representatives, Theo Rogers, John Phillips and J. Meredith Williams.

They sailed with their volunteer battalion from Southampton on Wednesday 14th February, 1900, on the Union Line troopship the S.S. 'Greek', along with 800 men of the King's Own Scottish Borderers, the Northamptonshire, Bedfordshire and Manchester Regiments, and they experienced all the awe and wonder known to all whose first venture outside their home boundaries has been to cross the seas in

Bound for the Cape: Below decks on a troopship, 1900. *(National Army Museum).*

their country's service. They wrote of the rough sea in the Bay of Biscay, when "from bow to stern the deck was covered with the troops and nothing but groans could be heard and all were in a helpless condition", and they told how King Neptune and his Court conducted the traditional ceremony for their first crossing of the equator. They told, too, of their first Saint David's day so far away from home, when:

> Every Welshman aboard was adorned with a leek in his cap and a huge leek had been put up in our quarters, underneath being the inscription 'Gwell Angeu na Chywilydd'. In the evening we had a grand concert with some grand singing and a chorus by the male voice party, which was very well rendered.

And then the thoughts of home:

> At 8 o'clock, which meant about 9 o'clock at home, Captain Philipps of the South Wales Borderers, in a neat speech, said that they all knew what they had congregated for that evening. At home several gatherings were being held and no doubt they at home were thinking about them, and he asked for three hearty cheers for their friends at home, which was heartily responded to.

The account of their memorable sixteen days voyage concluded in a manner which typified the wide-eyed innocence of boys journeying into places and experiences hitherto undreamed of:

> It is very pleasing to the eye on a dark night to watch the phosphorous on the sea and various fishes splashing on the water, leaving a trail of greenish hue behind them. Numerous fishes have been seen, from the flying fish to the huge whale.
>
> All have been served with a hundred rounds of ammunition each and we are ready and eager to go to the front. Now, as Capetown seems like a speck in the distance, we conclude our narrative, hoping that it has proved interesting to your readers [of the *Carmarthen Journal*], and as Saint Peter's Boys we can assure them that we will uphold the best traditions of the good and ancient town of Carmarthen.

Meanwhile, in "the good and ancient town of Carmarthen", as in the whole country, there was an atmosphere of disappointment and defeat as dispatch after dispatch from South Africa brought fresh news of Boer successes against the pride of Britain's army. But then, Mafeking was relieved. Throughout Great Britain the celebrations which greeted the news were on a scale out of all proportion to the significance of the event, such was the contrast between this small gleam of hope and the darkness of the backcloth against which it shone. The celebrations were unprecedented and became legendary, so much so that they even added a new word to the English Language, a word still in the dictionary, the verb 'Maffick'—to celebrate uproariously! Naturally, Carmarthen was not to be outdone by any Welsh town in terms of banners, bonfires, fireworks, music, processions, and that particular Carmarthen favourite, Cannon Fire. It was that that brought tragedy to the celebrations, when a cannon was being served and fired by several coraclemen on the Quay. The barrel exploded and jagged pieces of it crashed through the chest of one of them—thirty two years old John Williams, of 40 Mill Street—and killed him. At the Inquest, all his companions denied overloading the cannon with powder as a joke on Williams . . . and all vehemently denied being drunk. The verdict was "Accidental Death".

On the second day of the celebrations, when Guildhall Square was packed for an open air concert (for which Mr.

Coracleman John Williams, killed by the bursting barrel of a cannon being fired on Carmarthen Quay to celebrate the relief of Mafeking. *(Peter Thomas).*

Mr. Edward Colby Evans, who provided the musicial accompaniment for the Mafeking celebrations, from a piano mounted on a cart in Guildhall Square. *(Theo Rogers).*

Edward Colby Evans provided the accompaniment on a piano mounted on a cart), Mayor Walter Spurrell opened a fund for the widow and her four children, who had been left "in almost destitute circumstances", and among the first donations were the twelve Inquest Jurymen's fees of two shillings (10p) each, and two shillings each from Jack Williams' four grief-stricken fellow coraclemen.

## NOTES

[1]David Jones became the Force's first Inspector, and deputy to the Chief Constable. See *A Shilling for Carmarthen,* Chapter 11—'Poacher Turned Gamekeeper'.

[2]Uncle of Theo Rogers, Town Clerk of Carmarthen until his retirement in 1980.

[3]Nearly 450,000 British and Empire troops fought about 90,000 Boers, and while the British alone and the Boers each lost around 6,000 killed, 13,350 British troops died of disease and neglect. Shades of the 18,058 hospital deaths in the Crimea!

[4]Not the least of the causes of world condemnation was the use by the British General Kitchener of camps in which were placed tens of thousands of Boer women, children and other non-combatants in order to rob their fighting men of help and shelter. Under appalling maladministration, some 20,000 died in these places, for which the British had coined a new term . . . *Concentration Camps.*

[5]"It was very generally assumed that English fibre had been softened and disintegrated by prosperity. The poor show we had made in the Boer war had confirmed this idea." (*War Memoirs of David Lloyd George,* (Odhams Press Ltd., London, 1934).

[6]*With the Flag to Pretoria,* a popular magazine series published weekly by Harmsworth Bros. in 1900.

[7]He was so severely wounded that he was invalided to his father's home in Carmarthen.

[8]Khaki, a sand-coloured cloth, originated in the Indian army and was adopted by the British army for the second Boer war.

[9]*Carmarthen Journal.*

[10]Benjamin Rees was spared to return home safe to Carmarthen.

## A SOLDIER'S LIFE

Like all their comrades on the s.s. 'Greek' and all the other troopships pouring men into Capetown, the three Saint Peter's Boys were anxious to get to the front and have a go at the Boer before it was all over. They need not have worried. There was plenty of fight left in the Boer yet. Their letters and those of the other Carmarthenshire men fighting in South Africa would continue to fire the imagination of their fellow townsmen on long marches over veldt and river crossing, on hair-raising rail journeys hanging grimly on to flat waggons ready to fight their way out of Boer ambushes, over battlefields strewn with smoking wreckage and the freshly dead, following the Boer rearguard to Pretoria. When that final goal proved merely to mark the end of the "conventional" war and the beginning of a protracted guerilla war, they wrote home about that too, and the whole town read their letters.

A few extracts serve to show something of the rigours of nineteenth century soldiering, some of the climaxes and anti-climaxes of battle, and some of those chance encounters with friends that occur in wartime and that prove what a small world it really is:

Private Fred Davies, with 'H' Company of the 2nd Battalion, East Yorkshire Regiment: Writing to his father in Parade Road, Carmarthen, he describes a journey by rail to Kimberley, a journey broken for a time by the bridge at Norvalspont which had been blown up by the retreating Boers.

> I sat down on a box against a sentry and we got into conversation together. We were talking about ten minutes when I noticed the badge alongside of his helmet—The Welch Regiment. 'Oh' I said 'You belong to the Welch Regiment. What part of Wales do you come from?' and you should have seen the two of us when he said Carmarthen, and who should it be but Dai Owens, who used to live on the Parade.
>
> As we were coming up the line we stopped at a station. I forget the name of it now, but they have such comical names out here. There was a lot of soldiers on the platform cheering us and I asked them what they belonged to and they said the Welsh Volunteers. I asked them if they had any chaps from Carmarthen with them and one of them said 'Yes, I'll go and look for them' and who should they bring but Theo Rogers. We just had a few words together. We hardly knew one another, with our whiskers on. We have not shaved—and I don't think he has—since we started from England. We do look 'Proper Warriors'.
>
> I was pleased when he told me that Wales beat Ireland.

*　　*　　*

"On long marches over veldt and river crossing." The 41st (Welch) Regiment takes a rest, and some find time for a letter home. *(National Army Museum).*

Fred Davies again:

Dear Father, we leave here for Bloemfontein at 7 tonight and we expect a big fight on Monday or Tuesday, as the Boers are going to make a great final attack to retake Bloemfontein. There is a terrible lot of reinforcements going up and Lord Roberts has over 80,000 men with him. I am very pleased that we are with him. Dear Father, this is all. Excuse the writing as it is on the butt end of my rifle, so I will conclude with love to you all, from your ever affectionate son, Fred.

* * *

Private Alec Rees, of the 1st Battalion, Welch Regiment, writing from Bloemfontein to his father, David Rees, Tailor, Spilman Street:

Dear Father and Mother, I am taking the pleasure of writing you these few lines hoping to find you in the best of health, as I am at present. Dear Parents, I joined this Regiment on the 9th of April at a place called Norvalspont. Dear father and mother, I don't think it will last very much longer, so if I live to come home I will sleep for a month. I don't think I have any more at present, but give my love to Mr. Edwin Jones, Billy Reed and all the family and accept the same yourselves from your ever-loving son, Alec.

* * *

Trooper D. H. Lewis, describing how it felt to be under fire, with Thorneycroft's Mounted Infantry:

> How did I feel when first under fire? Well I really had no time to feel anything because I was under fire before I knew it. We were told to scale a kopje and when we got to the top, to my surprise a hail of bullets met us, and we were hard at it before we had time to think. I must say I never felt any fright, but when you know the night before that you have to fight an engagement at daybreak, you may get a little tugging at the heart and wonder whether you will pull through all right. Still, after the second or third fight, you lose all nervousness and go about your work as methodically as you would at a game of cricket.

* * *

Trooper Lewis maintains his cricketing metaphor:

> With regard to the battle of Colenso, well of course that's where I finished my innings. We were attacking Hwlangani Hill. We had been trying to storm it but failed and I had just brought in a wounded man and placed him in safety by some bushes. Being told that there was another man lying wounded between our position and the hill, I volunteered to go and fetch him. He could walk with assistance, so I simply took hold of his elbow and we both made for cover, and while crossing the open I suddenly felt a blow in the back. It was just for all the world as if someone had hit me with a brick or a large heavy stone. I fell on my knees. I told the other fellow that as he had managed to walk somehow, he had better hook it. He did so and I lay down flat. Presently I stretched my arms out and began to move my body a little to see how I was injured and whether I could walk, but being paralysed in the legs that was impossible, but as soon as I did so a hail of bullets came round me from the Boers, so I thought better to lay low for a while.
>
> In about half an hour an officer came round and finding me wounded called another officer, and they both dragged me by the arms, face downwards, to a bush close by and placed me behind it. While one of them was turning me over with the intention of bandaging me, a bullet struck him in the forehead and came out through the back of his head.
>
> How I got away from the field I do not quite remember.
>
> Our own doctors on the field refused to take the bullet out as my case was regarded as hopeless, and there were other more hopeful cases which needed immediate attention. One of them when he

looked at me shook his head and I happened to see him do so. I said to him 'You needn't shake your head doctor. I'm not going to pay out.'[1]

* * *

Private Theo Rogers, writing to his parents from Vet River Station, Orange Free State:

I expect you have been disappointed at not getting any letters from me these last two or three weeks, but really, we haven't had time to breathe.

Since we have been here we have done nothing only navvy's work, helping the engineers about the railways [they were still working their way to the front to join their Regiment] but after eight days of it I can tell you we are very tired of it. A large number of Boers came in yesterday and gave up their arms. The general opinion seems to be that the war is practically over and so we shall not see any fighting. If that is the case, the sooner it is over the better, for us to get from here to where there is more to eat. [The war was to go on for two years yet, and Theo Rogers, *did* see some fighting].

* * *

Private Johnnie Phillips, writing from Bloemfontein to a friend with the *Carmarthen Journal:*

Dear Old Bill; I am writing this letter to you from Bloemfontein. I left Capetown with the Welsh and we journeyed round Port Elizabeth and trained it from there to Springfontein, which took us two days. Here we received orders to disentrain. On Saturday week last [21st April, 1900] we received orders to march from there to Bloemfontein to provide an escort for a convoy, so at 3 a.m. the following morning we struck camp and started this march. The convoy was about two miles in length, drawn by oxen. We were marching before sunrise and after sunset, every night piling arms and sleeping alongside of them ready to move on again. We arrived at Bloemfontein yesterday morning, thus marching the 190 miles in a week exactly. Our Section was in charge of Colour Sergeant Ben Evans, Priory Street, who was returning to the front after having been wounded at Paardeburg.

* * *

Private Johnnie Phillips again:

Dear Father and Mother; Just a line or so to let you know that I am alive and well. I dare say you know that I have joined the Welch Regiment at the front. The Regiment is in the 19th Brigade under General Pole-Carew. The Division marched from Bloemfontein yesterday. We started at 7 o'clock, each man carrying a blanket, and we continued marching with two hours rest during the day, until 7 o'clock last night. I can tell you, we were all done up. We then camped for the night at a place called Karre, thus you can see that I have been lucky enough to take part in the general advance to Pretoria, and I hope I will be able to pull through all right. We all slept last night in the open air with our guns and everything else ready, with one blanket wrapped around us, and during the night it got wet through with the dew.

There are several Carmarthen chaps in the Regiment. Sorry to hear that the team had such a bashing with Swansea Seconds.

* * *

Johnnie Phillips, James Meredith Williams and Theo Rogers fought their way to Pretoria with the Welch Regiment in Lord Roberts' army. They fought in other actions after that, but became less active as the set-piece battle gradually gave way to the much more mobile guerilla warfare, and by May, 1901, a year before the end of the war, they were back in Old Carmarthen, to a heroes' welcome. With them came Sergeant Langman, another of the Carmarthen Volunteers, who had followed them out to South Africa a fortnight later.

The town went wild, and they were carried shoulder high from the railway station to Guildhall Square to a reception and speeches of welcome the like of which would have been reserved for none less than a General or an Admiral a century before, when Private Wheeler asked ". . . who shall record the glorious deeds of the soldier whose lot is numbered with the thousands in the ranks who live and die and fight in obscurity?" At the opening of that century, only Generals and Admirals were heroes; the common soldier was merely a statistic, regarded even by his own generals as "The scum of the earth".[2] At its close, he had a name, and he was a hero in his own right.

The climax of several days of celebration was a banquet at

Lord Roberts' army enters Pretoria, 5th June, 1900. *(National Army Museum).*

the Ivy Bush Royal Hotel, at which the President was Lieutenant General Sir James Hills-Johnes, G.C.B., V.C., of Dolau Cothi, near Carmarthen, who raised the toast to four ordinary soldiers. Sergeant Langman replied for all four:

> Mr. President, Mr. Mayor, Comrades and Gentlemen; I thank you for the very hearty manner in which you have responded to the last toast, so warmly proposed by our gallant President. We esteem it a great honour that a British General who has won such renown on fields of battle and, moreover, is so great a friend of our noble Commander-in-Chief, Lord Roberts, who has accompanied him for many a mile on the road, should preside at this gathering. We four are very thankful to him, and I may add to Colonel Picton-Evans and to our Captain for their very energetic remarks regarding ourselves, four humble units in the South African Field Force.
>
> It has been our great privilege to serve under two Sovereigns, first under the greatest and noblest Queen the world has ever known, who was greatly revered and deeply mourned by her soldiers, and secondly under her worthy son and successor His Majesty the King, in whom we have good reason to glory and who will always find us ready and willing to serve him.
>
> Words are inadequate to express our thanks for the very good

reception we have had and the magnificent mementoes which we have received, which will recall the rousing send-off we had from the old town. My comrades had already done three months service when I joined them outside Pretoria. They belonged to the 1st Volunteer Service Company and I went out with the reinforcing draft. I can tell you that the welcome I received when I joined them was most hearty. One thing I must refer to is to the comforts so generously sent out by the ladies and gentlemen of the town. They arrived at a time when they were sorely needed. I am sure Carmarthen holds a name second to none with the men of the Old 41st. Speaking for myself I was in some straits. I won't describe it quite (laughter), but I was quite set up by the presents I received in common with the men of the Regiment. Little did I think when I saw the articles exhibited in this room early last year that I should come in for a share of them.

To conclude, I beg to thank you most warmly for your very kind remarks and for the very kind and unanimous way in which you have treated us, and recognised our humble efforts on behalf of our Country. I feel sure I can answer for the four of us that we shall always be ready and willing to do our duty to our Country and to uphold the honour of Saint Peter's Boys (applause).

Just five years later, in May 1906, a memorial to the Carmarthenshire men killed in the South African War was dedicated in an impressive ceremony in Guildhall Square, the very heart of the old town. Major General W. H. Mackinnon, C.V.O., C.B., unveiled the monument, as men of the Old 41st, The Welch Regiment, bowed their heads and rested on their arms reversed.

The two panels on the monument are inscribed with thirty-seven names, and one night some years later, a local ex-soldier who had fought in South Africa and who had earned the nickname Buller, after the British General, was found lying very drunk and crying bitterly at its foot. When asked why he was crying, he pointed to the names inscribed on the panels and bewailed the fact that though he had fought as hard as any of them, *his name had been omitted!*

The unveiling of the Boer War Memorial, Guildhall Square, in May, 1906.
*(Carmarthen Journal).*

The Guildhall and the Boer War Memorial. *(George Davies, Cwmduad).*

## NOTES

[1]Trooper Lewis did not 'Pay out'. The bullet was removed from alongside his spine, *without anaesthetic,* and after lying paralysed for a further three days he began a slow recovery. He was brought back to Britain by hospital ship and invalided to Carmarthen.

[2]Speaking to Earl Stanhope, the Duke of Wellington said that his soldiers were ". . . the very scum of the earth. People talk of their enlisting from their fine military feeling. All stuff. No such thing. Some of our men enlist from having got bastard children, some for minor offences many more for drink; but you can hardly conceive such a set brought together, and it really is wonderful that we should have made them the fine fellows they are." (Notes on the conversations with the Duke of Wellington, 1888—quoted in *The Great Duke,* Sir Arthur Bryant, CH, (Collins, London, 1971).

# Carriages

"As if the old mail coach rate of eight miles an hour was not fast enough for the march of civilisation, the devil has been raised in the shape of steam to impel us at his own pace."

Robert Southey in the 1830s.

## CARRIAGES

In 1800, Carmarthen's population was about five thousand . . . three times that of a village nearly seventy miles to the east called Cardiff, and in the first decade of the nineteenth century Carmarthen was booming and its population expanding rapidly. Expanding trade and commerce demanded good communications and the River Towy, Carmarthen's main trading highway, was at its busiest, the ships crowding its quay and anchorages including as many as a dozen brigs from America. The Towy had been the highway to Wales' most important town since long before the Romans first ventured cautiously up the ten winding miles of tidal river to trade with the Celts. And even now, fourteen hundred years after the Romans had left Carmarthen, the town's isolation on the landward side was only just beginning to ease, and the roads of the early nineteenth century, still maintained by unreliable and amateur parish labour,[1] still attracted only the hardiest of travellers. They travelled mainly on horse-back or with horse-drawn waggons, or led pack-horses, much as their ancestors had travelled when 'Watch and Ward' had closed the town gates at sunset five hundred years before.

Even the mail coaches were relative newcomers to those rough, rock-strewn tracks. They had been introduced in the latter part of the eighteenth century as the country squires, using their new found wealth, sought communication with others of their social standing in the fashionable centres of England. By the first decade of the nineteenth century there was an extensive network of coach runs, and though the journeys were still arduous and lengthy, all the major towns of England and Wales could be reached. In 1812, for example, Mr. Bennett of Hereford extended his Brecon coach westwards as far as Carmarthen, putting within reach London, Gloucester, Bristol, Oxford, Worcester, Birmingham, Ludlow, Shrewsbury, Chester, Liverpool, Holyhead and all parts of the north of England. Leaving the Castle Inn at Brecon at five o'clock in the morning, his coaches made the fifty mile run to

One of Mr. Bennett's coaches? A mail coach on the Carmarthen to Cheltenham run. *(Carmarthen Museum. Photo by Doug Simpson).*

Carmarthen the same day, arriving late in the evening. He ran a thrice-weekly service, as did another company, who advertised their "New and Elegant Post Coach, carrying four inside only", running from the Bull and Mouth Inn, London, and taking two days to reach the Ivy Bush Inn, Carmarthen.

At the turn of the century, waggons were running from London to Carmarthen in ten days, and by around 1810 the weekly runs from Carmarthen to London, through Llandeilo, Llangadog, Llandovery, Brecon, Crickhowell, Abergavenny, Monmouth, Ross-on-Wye and Gloucester, linked with others to warehouses all over England. The tone of the advertisements of the time testifies to keen competition for passengers and goods.

Through the turnpike trusts, the gentry were using their influence and money to improve roads and bridges to expand this traffic, though the general state of the roads in south Wales as late as 1818 was so atrocious that the Postmaster General threatened to withdraw the Irish Mail service through Milford Haven altogether! Ten days for a horse-drawn waggon to travel from London was long enough, but the westward route to Pembrokeshire was barely passable; it could take a waggon seven hours to cover the five miles from Tavernspite to Narberth. The vulnerability of these services to winter weather

THE OLDEST, THE MOST

Expeditious, and Regular Conveyance

BY WAGGON,

*To and from* **LONDON** *and* **MILFORD,**

The direct Road through Abergavenny, Monmouth, Gloucester, Oxford, &c.

DAVID REES, CARRIER,

CARMARTHEN,

RETURNS his unfeigned thanks to his Friends and the Public in general, for the liberal encouragement he continues to receive, and begs leave to inform them, that the Connection he has lately formed from all parts of the North of England, enables him to deliver Goods in South Wales at a much lower rate than any other conveyance.

The Waggons, &c. set out from the undermentioned places, viz.

LONDON—From the Saracen's-Head Inn, Friday-street, every Saturday evening, per Heane, and arrive at Carmarthen the Monday morning se'nnight.

GLOUCESTER—From Heane's Warehouse, every Wednesday, per North.

MANCHESTER, and all Parts of the North of England—Per Pickford's Fly Boats, every Monday, Wednesday, and Friday, from Manchester to Worcester,—from thence per Rees and Co. who load at Howes and Co.'s Warehouse, Worcester, every Wednesday, for all parts of South Wales.

N. B.—All Goods from Nottingham, Coventry, Leicester, Birmingham, Bewdley, Kidderminster, &c. &c. are particularly requested to be directed by Rees and Co. from Worcester,—from whence they may depend on receiving them, in five days, in Carmarthen, and at a reduced price.

☞ No money, plate, jewels, watches, writings, glass, china, wearing-apparel, &c. will be accounted for, unless entered as such, and paid for accordingly.

Carmarthen, April 17, 1817.

D. R. has just laid in a Stock of prime Porter, Brown Stout and Bottled Porter, which is now on sale, in Barrels, Kilderkins, and Hampers, on the most reasonable terms.

By waggon to London in 10 days, 1817.
*(Carmarthen Journal).*

IVY-BUSH INN, CARMARTHEN,

*APRIL* 11, 1815.

THE Public are most respectfully informed, that A NEW LIGHT POST-COACH, CALLED

THE GENERAL PICTON,

Leaves CARMARTHEN for SWANSEA, through Kidwelly and Llanelly, every Monday, Wednesday, & Friday, at two o'clock in the afternoon: and Passengers and Parcels will be forwarded from Swansea by the Bristol Day Coach, at four o'clock on the following mornings. Returns from the Mackworth-Arms, Swansea, every Tuesday, Thursday, and Saturday morning at eight o'clock, and will forward Passengers and Parcels, arriving in Swansea by the Bristol Day Coach of the preceding evenings.

After the 12th of May next, THE GENERAL PICTON COACH will proceed immediately from CARMARTHEN to TENBY, and return from thence the following days, in time to depart for Swansea at the above hour.

Passengers and Parcels may be booked at either of the before-mentioned towns for Bristol.

The Proprietors will not be accountable for any Parcel above the value of Five Pounds, unless entered and paid for accordingly.

The 'General Picton' coach, 1815.
*(Carmarthen Journal).*

can be judged by the experience of the severe winter of 1814, when the last coach to get through before snow isolated Carmarthen for many days, arrived from London four days late! It was said at the time that:

> . . . the heavy falls of snow in the Principality have not here been surpassed during the last fifty years, and navigation of the River Towy has for some weeks been completely obstructed by the ice, which was not only sufficiently solid to support skaters, but to furnish the youthful ramblers of this town and neighbourhood with a promenade of about two miles in length.

This was isolation indeed, for even when the winter was less severe, the coaches were at the mercy of flood and quagmire, and the sailing ships at the mercy of storm and adverse winds whatever the season, until well into the century.

By the 1830s the railway age was still twenty years away from Carmarthen (though there was talk of a railway being planned to link London with Bristol),[2] but the improved state of the roads brought about by the turnpike trusts in the early years of the century had already put Carmarthen in more frequent and closer contact with other important towns. At the same time, though, the abuses of the turnpike system which were eventually to incur the wrath of Rebecca were already to be seen. The town's magistrates frequently dealt with cases of over-charging, as when they issued a warning to gatekeepers in general when fining William Williams, keeper of the Water Street gate, after Mr. Davies of Trawsmawr (a Magistrate) had complained that Williams had demanded and taken from him two full tolls within twenty-four hours, a breach of the rule laid down by the turnpike laws. Williams was lucky that in this instance the aggrieved traveller sought redress from the law, because in the last quarter of 1833 Carmarthen's magistrates' court was full of cases of assaults on gate-keepers by less tolerant complainants!

The number of toll-gates would before long grow to become an intolerable burden on the country people, and Carmarthen's Water Street gate was to loom large in the Rebecca riots,[3] but it must be said that it was to those same turnpike trusts that the coach operators and the travelling public owed the greatly improved state of the roads.

Mail coaches now left the Post Office in Spilman Street twice a day for London, and one left at four o'clock every morning to catch the Irish packet boat from Milford, while passenger coaches were in and out of Carmarthen throughout the day to and from all points of the compass, at least twelve a day arriving at the Ivy Bush Inn. The town's crack coach services were provided by the Regulator and the Cambrian coaches, based at the Ivy Bush and the Boar's Head respectively. Leaving the Angel Inn at Cardigan at seven in the morning and calling only at the Salutation Tavern, Newcastle Emlyn, the Regulator would arrive at one o'clock in Carmarthen ". . . from whence there are mails and post coaches daily to all parts of the Kingdom".

The stage coach and the fly waggon (for freight) were still Carmarthen's shortest link with Bristol, but with the arrival of steamships on the Bristol Channel in the 1920s it became apparent that it would be quicker to get to Bristol by taking the road west, to Pembrokeshire. The Cambrian coach was introduced in May, 1830, to connect with the increasingly numerous coastal paddle steamers calling at Tenby, a combined service which greatly outpaced even the Bristol Mail coaches. Aberystwyth was now some twelve hours away by the Collegian coach, which ran three times a week via Lampeter and Aberaeron. Other local coach services to and from the Ivy Bush Inn were the Picton, daily for Swansea, taking five and a half hours to get there via Kidwelly and Llanelli, and the Regulator, three times a week for Tenby and Haverfordwest.

And the railway age was now within reach, by the Monarch coach, which travelled to Birmingham in one day, to convey passengers to the Birmingham, Manchester and Liverpool Railway. The Paul Pry coach provided the fastest service from the Ivy Bush to London (in twenty six hours) at single fares of £3.12s.0d. [£3.60] inside and £1.16s.0d. [£1.80] outside.[4] Cheltenham was fourteen hours away, and passengers could sleep there, catch the Magnet coach to Maidenhead next morning and proceed to London from there on the Great Western Railway.

The General Post Office in Spilman Street reported that its business had:

> . . . materially increased in consequence of the great facilities now afforded to publishers of printed books, magazines, reviews,

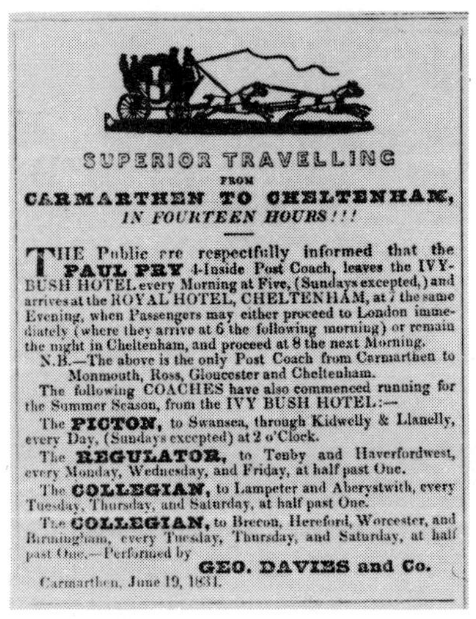

SUPERIOR TRAVELLING
FROM
CARMARTHEN TO CHELTENHAM,
*IN FOURTEEN HOURS!!!*

THE Public are respectfully informed that the **PAUL PRY** 4-Inside Post Coach, leaves the IVY-BUSH HOTEL every Morning at Five, (Sundays excepted,) and arrives at the ROYAL HOTEL, CHELTENHAM, at 7 the same Evening, when Passengers may either proceed to London immediately (where they arrive at 6 the following morning) or remain the night in Cheltenham, and proceed at 8 the next Morning.

N.B.—The above is the only Post Coach from Carmarthen to Monmouth, Ross, Gloucester and Cheltenham.

The following COACHES have also commenced running for the Summer Season, from the IVY BUSH HOTEL:—

The **PICTON,** to Swansea, through Kidwelly & Llanelly, every Day, (Sundays excepted) at 2 o'Clock.

The **REGULATOR,** to Tenby and Haverfordwest, every Monday, Wednesday, and Friday, at half past One.

The **COLLEGIAN,** to Lampeter and Aberystwith, every Tuesday, Thursday, and Saturday, at half past One.

The **COLLEGIAN,** to Brecon, Hereford, Worcester, and Birmingham, every Tuesday, Thursday, and Saturday, at half past One.—Performed by

**GEO. DAVIES and Co.**

Carmarthen, June 19, 1834.

Fourteen hours to Cheltenham, and twenty-five to London, 1834.
*(Carmarthen Journal).*

prints, maps &c., and to the public at large to forward them to and from every part of the United Kingdom through the post—at the rate of sixpence [2½p] per pound or any part thereof.

Heavily loaded mail coaches clattered to and from the office throughout the day, to and from Bristol, Gloucester and London and all the towns of South West Wales. And there were four deliveries of mail a day in Carmarthen itself.[5]

NOTES

[1] The day per year required of every man in the Parish accomplished so little that it was regarded as a day off. Hence the expression, still in use to this day, "A day for the King (or Queen)", meaning a day off work.

[2] As early as 1825 (and he was still campaigning in 1831), a London man named Fortune called for a railroad between London and Bristol, to make Bristol "the most important port in the British Empire" and to supply London with coal from Wales "at half the present price". He also proposed a railroad from London to Birmingham and one, through Gloucester, to Wales. In the latter, he was 27 years before his time!

[3] See *A Shilling for Carmarthen,* chapter 5—'Beca'.

[4] Ten years later, competition had brought these fares down by one-fifth.

[5] Only 16 years before, in 1822, there was one collection daily for London and Ireland, and posts on four days a week to the West Wales towns.

## THE IRON ROAD

The coach connections with the railway at Birmingham and Maidenhead in 1838 were Carmarthen's first contact with the railway age, at a time when the newspapers were full of prospectuses for the formation of railway companies and for the promotion of Parliamentary Bills for the purpose. The newspapers of Wales also carried eagerly-awaited news of the westward extension of the Iron Road . . . almost a yard-by-yard commentary.[1]

In the short space of thirteen or fourteen years the railway progressed from Maidenhead to Oxford, to Gloucester, Chepstow, Newport, Cardiff and to Swansea—tantalisingly close, but even there bringing London to within a little over twelve hours of Carmarthen. Within those thirteen or fourteen years the journey to London from Carmarthen had already been cut by thirty-six hours!

London is brought to within a little over 12 hours of Carmarthen. Swansea railway station opens in 1850. *(National Library of Wales).*

By June 1851 the integration of the stage coaches with the railway could be seen in advertisements like this:

> Communication between Swansea, Tenby and Aberystwyth: The public is respectfully informed that the Company's four-horse summer coaches will run as follows during the season, from Swansea to Tenby—
>
> The Hero coach will leave the Mackworth Arms Hotel and Railway Station at 11 a.m., after the arrival of the 10.45 down train [from London], passing through Llanelli, Kidwelly, Carmarthen and Saint Clears, arriving at Tenby at 7 p.m. every Monday, Wednesday and Friday, returning the alternate days, leaving the White Lion Hotel [Tenby] at 5 a.m., arriving in Swansea in time for the 1 p.m. train up to Chepstow.
>
> From Swansea to Aberystwyth: The Hero coach from the Mackworth Arms Hotel and Railway Station at 9 a.m., passing through Llanelli, Kidwelly, Carmarthen, Lampeter and Aberaeron, arriving in Aberystwyth at 9 p.m. every Tuesday, Thursday and Saturday, returning from the Belle Vue Hotel, Aberystwyth, at 7 a.m. every Monday, Wednesday and Friday, arriving in Swansea in time for the 7 p.m. train to London.

Elaborating on this announcement, the *Carmarthen Journal* took the opportunity to remind its readers of the facilities of the Ivy Bush Coaching Establishment, directing their attention to:

THE GREAT WESTERN RAILWAY

IS now open for the conveyance of Passengers, Horses, and Carriages, from GLOUCESTER to LONDON, and all intermediate Stations.

☞ Full particulars can be obtained, and handbills of the time of departure of the Trains sent by post on application to the Superintendant at Gloucester, or at any of the other Stations on the line.

The Great Western Railway from London reaches Gloucester, 1845.
*(Carmarthen Journal).*

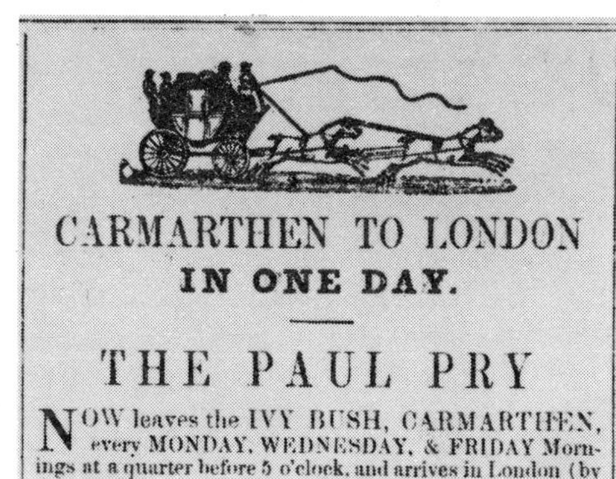

CARMARTHEN TO LONDON
IN ONE DAY.

THE PAUL PRY

NOW leaves the IVY BUSH, CARMARTHEN, every MONDAY, WEDNESDAY, & FRIDAY Mornings at a quarter before 5 o'clock, and arrives in London (by the Great Western Railway from Gloucester) same evening at 10 o'clock.

The 'Paul Pry' coach connects Carmarthen with the Great Western Railway at Gloucester.
*(Carmarthen Journal).*

THE Public is respectfully informed, that the OLD COMPANY'S RAILWAY COACH will leave the Mackworth Arms Railway Station every morning after the arrival of the 10 45 A.M. Down Train for Carmarthen, Haverfordwest, and Tenby, returning the same evening for the London Mail Train, 5 15. P.M., at
EXTRAORDINARY LOW FARES.
For further particulars, enquire at the Ivy Bush Coach-Office, Carmarthen.

The Mackworth Arms, Swansea, where stage coach and train meet.
*(Carmarthen Journal).*

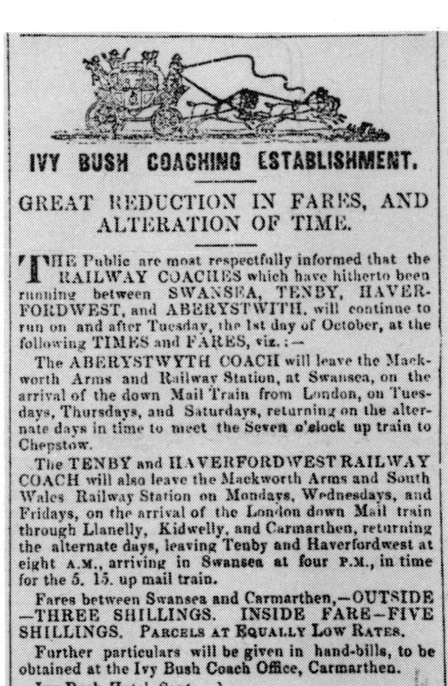

**IVY BUSH COACHING ESTABLISHMENT.**

GREAT REDUCTION IN FARES, AND ALTERATION OF TIME.

THE Public are most respectfully informed that the RAILWAY COACHES which have hitherto been running between SWANSEA, TENBY, HAVERFORDWEST, and ABERYSTWITH, will continue to run on and after Tuesday, the 1st day of October, at the following TIMES and FARES, viz.:—

The ABERYSTWYTH COACH will leave the Mackworth Arms and Railway Station, at Swansea, on the arrival of the down Mail Train from London, on Tuesdays, Thursdays, and Saturdays, returning on the alternate days in time to meet the Seven o'clock up train to Chepstow.

The TENBY and HAVERFORDWEST RAILWAY COACH will also leave the Mackworth Arms and South Wales Railway Station on Mondays, Wednesdays, and Fridays, on the arrival of the London down Mail train through Llanelly, Kidwelly, and Carmarthen, returning the alternate days, leaving Tenby and Haverfordwest at eight A.M., arriving in Swansea at four P.M., in time for the 5. 15. up mail train.

Fares between Swansea and Carmarthen,—OUTSIDE—THREE SHILLINGS. INSIDE FARE—FIVE SHILLINGS. PARCELS AT EQUALLY LOW RATES.

Further particulars will be given in hand-bills, to be obtained at the Ivy Bush Coach Office, Carmarthen.

Ivy Bush Hotel, Sept., 26th, 1850.

The Ivy Bush Coaching Establishment. *(Carmarthen Journal).*

. . . the great accommodation which this celebrated company offer in the means of travelling between Aberystwyth, Tenby and Swansea.

The Hero is a most well-appointed coach and keeps most excellent time, and travels through most delightful country abounding with the most romantic and beautiful scenery. We doubt not that the spirited exertions of the proprietors will secure for them a fair share of public patronage.

And then the ultimate in integrated coach and railway communication from Carmarthen, and the penultimate step towards a direct rail link. The *Carmarthen Journal* had:

. . . much pleasure in announcing the opening of the line from Swansea to Gloucester this day [Friday the 19th of September, 1851]. We understand that the Company have entered into a contract for conveying goods and passengers by boat across the river at Chepstow pending the completion of the bridge, so that very little inconvenience will be felt by this short break in the line. Coaches in connection with the express train from Swansea will also run from Carmarthen daily, thus bringing our town in direct communication with the Metropolis in the short space of ten hours.

Carmarthen was thus in the heyday of the stage-coach and on the threshold of the railway age, and it may be worth pausing here to look at the 'road traffic problems' of the day. It is not surprising, given the inherent congestion in the town, that accidents were frequent, and often fatal, as pedestrians (and particularly children) got under the wheels of the carts and carriages and under the feet of the horses, a situation not helped by the propensity of Carmarthenshire drivers and riders for "furious driving". The records show that Lammas Street and Guildhall Square were particular "race-tracks", where pedestrians took their lives in their hands—without benefit of Highway Code! Many were the cases where drink provided the additional motive power, and many were the complaints aired in the courts and the council chamber. And, as ever, the police were in the forefront of the argument:

Town Hall, 15th June, 1849: After several cases of furious driving in the town, in one of which it was alleged that the horses were going at the rate of *eight or nine miles an hour,* Mr. W. Morris observed that he had come down to the Hall for the purpose of making a complaint against the Police for not preventing furious driving. He was glad, however, that the Police had brought the parties to justice, as the nuisance of furious driving was a most intolerable one and exceedingly dangerous.

On Monday morning the driving through the streets was such as to place the lives of persons passing at the time in imminent jeopardy, as the carts were driving through the streets at a fearful rate. All the magistrates expressed it as their determination to do all in their power to abate the evil.

A report of a road accident in Spilman Street in October, 1851, contained another pointed reference to "furious driving", this time with a comment on the quality of the coach drivers of the day:

Coach accident in Spilman Street: An accident which might have been attended with very serious consequences occurred on Monday last to a posting chariot of Mr. Bowers of Tenby. The chariot, which was very heavily laden with passengers from Pembrokeshire, was driven by a son of Mr. Bowers and a postillion, and on turning the corner at the end of Queen Street the wheels came into contact with the kerbstone and the chariot fell on its side, throwing the passengers in different directions into the street. A crowd of people soon collected and the injured passengers were speedily removed and every attention paid to them by J. Hughes, Esquire, Surgeon, and the parties to whose houses they were taken.

We hope this accident will have a beneficial effect on those reckless drivers who too often expose the lives of their passengers to imminent danger.

An accident to a Carmarthen-based stage coach (and there were many of them) would receive fulsome treatment in the local press, especially when there was loss of life. And the report would frequently conclude with a reference to the coachman's well-known partiality to the jug:

Coach accident and loss of life: An accident which was attended with loss of life occurred on Friday 25th of May, [1849] to the Cardigan Mail Coach on its journey from Carmarthen to Cardigan, when at a short distance beyond Newcastle Emlyn. There were four persons, including the coachman and horsekeeper, outside, and two persons, inside, viz. Mr. Morgan Jenkins, a very respectable draper residing in Cardigan, and his daughter.

When near the post office in Newcastle Emlyn, a drunken man got up behind and refused to go down or to pay his fare. The coachman, a person named William Evans, who occasionally drives and is the landlord of the Railway Tavern in Bridge Street, Carmarthen, endeavoured to get him off by a pretty free use of the whip. Eventually, when near the old turnpike gate, the man got off and commenced running after the coach, catching hold of it behind. The coachman got down to make him let go his hold, which having succeeded in doing, he again took his seat on the box, whipped the horses so as to get away from the man and then looked back. This occurred as the coach was going down a steep hill, and while the coachman was looking back the coach ran up against a wall at the side of the road and was upset.

The outside passengers were all thrown off, but were not materially injured. Mr. Jenkins, who was inside, cried out for assistance, and as soon as the outside passengers got up, the coachman and another passenger proceeded to extricate him, but could not until the coach was righted. This having been done, Mr. Jenkins was taken out and placed with his back against the hedge, but it was found he was dead.

> It is said the coachman was intoxicated at the time. We trust that in future no person will be allowed to hold such a responsible situation as that of driver of a coach unless he is a man of sober and careful habits—especially that one who has been taken off the box as a person unfit to have the lives of persons under his charge by reason of drunkenness will not again be permitted to perform such a responsible duty.

In the coaching trade, as in many other walks of life in Carmarthen in those days, drunkenness was rife!

But the writing was on the wall for the long-haul Carmarthen stage coaches, as the railway snaked its way from Swansea, through Llanelli and around the eastern estuaries of Carmarthen Bay. Carmarthen was approaching her most significant milestone.

As early as 1846 the South Wales Railway Company had its eye on Carmarthen, and in March of that year it was noted that:

> The surveyors on this line have for the past week been busily engaged in the neighbourhood of this town in marking out the ground required for the proposed line. We believe there is no doubt that the work will be speedily commenced.

They were right. Three years later the line had entered its last lap as the railhead reached the Towy Estuary, ten miles away from Carmarthen, with an urgency which evoked the comment that:

> The works on the South Wales Railway in this neighbourhood are now being carried on with increased energy, particularly on that portion of the line between this town and Kidwelly, between which places there are full five hundred men at work. The sea wall on the sands at the Ferry is progressing rapidly and fresh hands are continually being engaged to expedite the work. On the sands, where it was feared by some that a good foundation could not be obtained unless at a great depth, an excellent bottom of rock and in some places shingle has been got at about nine feet from the surface. It is calculated that about a hundred tons of the rocks at the Ferry have been blasted every day.

Even though the railway was not to reach Carmarthen for another three years and Swansea would remain the nearest railhead town until then, the railway's nearness was already bringing long-distance travel within the reach of, if not exactly the masses, then a considerably larger body of its people than ever before. The middle class and a growing number of wage-earning 'mechanics' in Carmarthen could now contemplate travel to an extent undreamed of only a very few years before, and the best example of this was symbolic in a wider sense, involving as it did the Great Exhibition of 1851.

Opened on the 1st of May, 1851, in the Crystal Palace in Hyde Park, London, by Queen Victoria, whose Consort, Prince Albert, was its patron, this great international event proclaimed to the world Britain's predominance in the industrial revolution and her growing power and influence on the world stage. It was seen as symbolising above all the dawn of a new age in which everyone—rich and poor, privileged and exploited, master and mechanic—were to share. Its accessibility to people from all quarters of the Kingdom by that dynamic of the industrial revolution, the railways, was appreciated early in Carmarthen, where, at a meeting held in the Lion Royal Hotel in Spilman Street on the 28th of February, 1851, a Grand Exhibition Society was formed, with the object of "arranging a pleasant and economical trip among themselves to London in the Autumn of the present year in order to pay a visit to the Great Industrial Exhibition of all Nations". They also had something in mind for those less able to find the money for the trip:

> One of the principal features of the Society is also to obtain funds by means of donations and subscriptions to enable them to send as many as possible of the clever and deserving mechanics of Carmarthen to London to visit the Exhibition, either free of expense or to afford them some partial assistance from the funds so obtained, which the Society considers will not only be affording a great gratification to the industrious artisans of Carmarthen and its immediate neighbourhood, but may eventually lead to still more beneficial results, such as the cultivation of taste, the improvement of the mind, and be a stimulant to industry, and which it is also hoped will operate as an incentive to emulation and may eventually be the means of leading to distinction and honour.

There was indeed "distinction and honour", for two Carmarthen tradesmen actually received awards at the Great Exhibition:

> Mr. Richard Davies, Hatter, Shaw's Lane, and Mr. Richard

Istance, Cabinet Maker, Blue Street, received bronze medals, and certificates bearing the signature of H.R.H. Prince Albert and the Jurors' Reports [on their exhibits] beautifully bound.

But their journeys still involved a coach trip to Swansea and a boat crossing of the River Wye at Chepstow, and the final forging of the whole link was still eagerly awaited. All Carmarthen eyes were on the earthworks alongside the River Towy at Ferryside, when, suddenly, the shanty-town which housed the army of itinerant labourers there exploded in riot and fire as the long-standing hostility between the English and Welsh and the Irish reached flash point.

The spark was provided by a Saturday night fight in the Mariners' Inn in Ferryside village, which led to the place being wrecked and the landlord being kicked unconscious. The crowd around the pub quickly swelled as men ran from the railhead shanty-town carrying blazing brands and an assortment of weapons to join in what became a pitched battle. As men collapsed with knife wounds and broken limbs, the English and Welsh turned their attention to the shacks and tents occupied by the Irish and their families and the houses in the village in which many of them lodged, driving out the occupants and setting the places on fire. The glare of the fires and torches illuminated a night of terror, and even daylight brought no respite. By Monday, nine men had been stabbed, a much larger number otherwise injured, and between two and three hundred Irish men, women and children had been driven out of the smouldering railhead, most of them into Carmarthen, where a large number of them were seen "lounging about the streets of the town in a state of great destitution".

Even the expulsion of the Irish was not the end of the affair. For a fortnight there was sporadic rioting and wounding, and only a large and determined police operation under the command of Carmarthenshire's Chief Constable, Captain Scott, involving many special constables from Carmarthen town finally brought a kind of peace to the little riverside village of Ferryside and the much larger shanty town about the railhead.

Once peace was restored, work was quickly underway again. In February, 1852, tenders were invited for the building of stations at Carmarthen, Ferryside, Kidwelly, Pembrey,

Llanelli and Loughor, while only three months later it was reported that:

> The permanent way [the track] is being laid down in the neighbourhood of Ferryside. Materials for the station near this town are prepared and the greater portion deposited near the site. The building will now be speedily erected.

Two months more and Brunel's bridge over the Wye was opened, putting Swansea in uninterrupted rail communication with London. This huge metal tubular-suspension bridge, spanning eight hundred feet of water, and designed by that master railway engineer Isambard Kingdom Brunel, had cost £65,000.

And then, at about half past one in the afternoon of Monday the 6th of September, 1852, a vast crowd witnessed the arrival in Carmarthen of the very first engine to traverse the single track from Swansea. Belching thick black smoke and clouds of sparks, the tall-chimneyed monster pulled its trucks to the end of the track at an astonishing fifteen miles an hour! The great majority of those in the welcoming crowd were terror struck by the apparition. Fifteen miles an hour! The fastest thing they had ever seen or even imagined before that moment had been a galloping horse!

NOTES

[1]In 1845, during what was called the period of railway mania, Parliament granted powers for the construction of 2,883 miles of new railways to companies having a total capital of £44 millions. "For a time", it was said, "it seemed to be a national article of faith that the capacity of the country to absorb new railway schemes and make them profitable was unlimited." From an eventual peak of some 50,000 miles of route, the network has been reduced to its present total of around 11,000 miles.

## The Mighty Power of Steam

But the really great day arrived on Friday the 17th of September, 1852, and a special celebratory issue of the *Carmarthen Journal* captured the sense of history which excited every man, woman and child in the town. The editorial comment conveys this, and underlines the uniqueness of this event in the history of Carmarthen, even as viewed from the present day. Things would never be the same again.

> The Great and Important Event of opening that portion of the South Wales Railway between Swansea and Carmarthen has been long anticipated with feelings of deep interest and enthusiasm by the inhabitants of this and the adjoining Counties.
>
> This event is unquestionably without parallel in the history of Carmarthenshire. With the railway, a new and brighter era dawns upon Wales. Facility of communication only was required to raise the Principality to an equality with other parts of Her Majesty's Dominions. The illimitable mineral wealth that lies embedded in its mountains, its rich and fertile valleys, its ports—some of them the finest and best in the world—needed the 'Mighty Power of Steam' to raise this country, so richly endowed, to that eminence nature had evidently fitted it to occupy.
>
> The people, too, possessing faculties of the highest order with indomitable perseverance, required only the impulse and stimulus which the railway always gives, to develop those latent powers and place them far abovc their compeers.

The progress of the ceremonial train was savoured in all its detail:

> The start from Swansea: The 'New Era' which was to plant its footsteps to the westward dawned at an early hour at Swansea. Long before the hour named for starting—12 o'clock—the street leading to the railway presented an animated appearance, and about 11 o'clock the station was literally besieged. There was a tremendous rush—in fact such a scramble for seats was never witnessed before at Swansea. By a little after 12, however, the excitement had subsided, Mr. Clarke, the indefatigable superintendent of the line having kindly furnished a sufficient number of carriages.
>
> When all had been seated, a shrill whistle reverberated through the station, and off the monster train started, to Landore, where the Directors' train, in which Mr. Talbot M.P. and the Directors, as well as the band of the 48th Regiment, were seated, waiting for the train from Swansea.
>
> At Landore the inhabitants mustered stongly. There were the three engines, puffing and shrieking over the line, whilst the military band played a Welsh air, to the great gratification of the spectators. After a display of about ten minutes, during which the engines took up their respective stations—the train being propelled by three powerful engines, the Ganymede, the Pearl and the

'Ganymede'—one of the three engines that brought the first passenger train into Carmarthen on 17th September, 1852.

Caliban, which were gaily dressed—away we started for Loughor.

At this ancient borough, hundreds of spectators in their holiday attire greeted the train whilst 'The Flag that braved a thousand years in the battle and the breeze' floated triumphantly from the once proud turrets of Loughor. Mr. Williams presented a formal address to the directors of the South Wales Railway. Having passed over Loughor Bridge, which is a very substantial structure, Llanelli loomed in the distance and was approached in a few minutes.

The vicinity of Llanelli was truly gay. The inhabitants turned out en masse to welcome the train. The shipping were decked with their gayest buntings; the cannon roared, whilst the triumphal arches, interspersed with floral devices and welcome inscriptions, crossed the 'New Iron Road' in various places. The lively strains of the Military and Llanelli bands, too, fell gratefully on the ear. When the train stopped, the Directors' carriage was detached and a congratulatory address was presented to the Chairman and Directors. This having been replied to by Mr. Talbot in appropriate terms, the party left in splendid style amidst the most deafening shouts for Pembrey, where the Directors received a very cordial reception.

At Kidwelly, the most extensive preparations were made. The Mayor and Corporation, headed by the Deputy Recorder, Mr.

Jeffries, met the Directors at the station. Mr. Talbot and the Directors then partook of luncheon and after doing justice to a few refreshing glasses of champagne they returned to their carriage, and then left amidst the roar of cannon and the cheers of hundreds of the inhabitants.

The Ferryside. This was the next station reached, and it is but justice to the good folks of this charming place that they vied, and vied successfully too, with every station on the line. The preparations made here were very extensive and a vast deal of gunpowder was exhausted, and the inhabitants were most enthusiastic in greeting the Directors.[1]

The train was again on the move, and after a pleasant excursion along the Towy the train arrived at its place of destination—Carmarthen—where they were received by the most deafening cheers.

The train consisted of twenty carriages, and on its approach to the station it had a pleasing effect. It contained a large number of the Directors, ladies and gentlemen, and the band of the 48th Regiment. As soon as the train stopped, a general rush was made in the direction of the town, and the road was a perfect stream of people. A procession was formed and it proceeded direct to the Market Place, where a large shed had been fitted up for the occasion by Mr. J. L. Collard, the Markets Superintendent. It had a commodious and really handsome appearance and the universal opinion was that places of far greater pretensions had not been fitted up so well.

The Chairman, W. Morris, Esq., the Directors and several other gentlemen sat on a platform at one end. Over the Presidential chair were the words Victoria Regina and a star very beautifully done with coloured dahlias. The tables groaned beneath the rich load of delicacies that covered them. There were upwards of 800 persons present and so admirable were the arrangements that no disorder or unpleasantness occurred. Everyone was well supplied. The champagne was of the finest and best description, and many toasts were drunk.

There was a magnificent ball in the evening in a large marquee in a garden at the back of the Ivy Bush. There were three handsome chandeliers suspended from the roof and the band of the 48th Regiment and a Quadrille Band were in attendance. The ball was numerously and fashionably attended. Dancing was kept up with spirit until a late hour.

Thus had history been made, and the people made the most of their new-found mobility:

South Wales Railway: On Monday last [the 11th of October, 1852] the railway to this town was opened for public traffic. The first train started at half past six in the morning and there was a good sprinkling of people there to witness it. Since that time it has been running at stated periods. It is really astonishing what large numbers of people have, during the week, travelled over the line. We do not refer to those who, from the different towns on the line merely travelled for the novelty of the thing, but the through passenger traffic has been great for the first week, and the foreshadowing of what is anticipated.

Omnibusses, cabs, etc., are rattling their way through the streets to the station from an early hour in the morning until late at night. This has imparted an unwonted bustle and excitement to the town.

Within a few days of the triumphal opening of the line, a small advertisement appeared in the *Carmarthen Journal.* It was placed by Mrs. Jones, of the Mackworth Arms, Swansea, whose coaches, it will be remembered, had filled the gap between the railhead at Swansea and the towns to the west. And nothing could have better signalled the end of one era and the beginning of another:

To Coach Proprietors, Job and Postmasters, Farmers, Dealers and the Public: Mr. P. Thomas has the honour to announce that he has been instructed by Mrs. Jones to sell by auction at the stables of the Mackworth Arms, above thirty excellent, well-conditioned Coach, Job, Hack and Draught Horses, principally in daily work on her Mail Contracts, shortly to expire, together with several vehicles, a quantity of harness, &c. &c.

As soon as the new line was opened, the trains began to run regularly—five a day in each direction on the single line and many more when the second track was opened four months later. London was now only ten and a half hours away, Llanelli fifty minutes, Swansea an hour and twenty-five minutes and Cardiff three and a half hours, by scheduled passenger trains.[2]

Within a month, another bit of history was made:

Caution to Railway Travellers: On Wednesday last a man named Vaughan, servant of Mr. Douglas, Auctioneer, Llanelli, was brought up before Daniel Prytherch Esquire in the Guildhall, Carmarthen, charged with having travelled from Llanelli to Carmarthen over the railway without the requisite ticket.

The first passenger train approaches Carmarthen. *(National Library of Wales).*

"Carmarthen, where they were received by the most deafening cheers." 17th September, 1852. *(National Library of Wales).*

Mr. Hancorne, who appeared for the railway company, did not wish to press the charge as it was the first offence on the line. The full penalty for this offence is forty shillings [£2].

Following in rapid succession on the opening of the line came a goods service for the conveyance of "Merchandise and cattle between Carmarthen and Swansea and Paddington and all the principal stations on this line of railway", and special excursions to such events as the Gloucester and Birmingham Musical Festivals. For twenty-eight shillings [£1.40p] 1st class or twenty-two shillings and sixpence [£1.12½p] in other [closed] carriages, the people of Carmarthen could travel on

A cheap excursion train to London and Windsor: On Monday the 9th August [1853] an excursion train will leave Carmarthen at 6 a.m., calling at Pembrey, Llanelli, Swansea, Neath, Port Talbot, Bridgend, Cardiff, Newport, Chepstow, reaching Gloucester at 11.40 and Paddington about 4.30 p.m. The train will return from Paddington at 8 a.m. on the 10th.

And all this only twenty months after the navvies had rioted in the muddy earthworks and village of Ferryside, with not a railway sleeper yet laid in those earthworks!

It was a remarkably safe line given the technology of the time and the speed of its construction, because it remained accident free for five years. When the first accident did come, it seems the train was full of barristers, policemen and others travelling to the Carmarthen Summer Assizes!

A serious accident on the South Wales Railway and providential escape: On Friday last [10th July, 1857] the express train due here at 4.46 p.m. ran off the rails when nearly under the second bridge from Myrtle Hill Station and about 400 yards from Pibwr Wen. It appears that the engine got off the rails and ran along the line for about 125 yards, dragging the carriages after it, but the coupling chain fortunately breaking caused the engine and tender to run down the embankment with immense force, ploughing up the earth most fearfully, and the carriages after going for about 20 yards further on ran along the embankment and then quietly tumbled over against the boundary railings.

There were about thirty passengers in the train, but fortunately none of them were at all injured beyond a rather severe shaking. Among the passengers in the train at the time were Captain Scott [the Chief Constable of Carmarthenshire] and his family, James

Captain Scott, Chief Constable of Carmarthenshire, survived Carmarthen's first train crash while en-route to Carmarthen Assizes, 10th July, 1857.

*(Carmarthen Museum).*

Bowen, Henry Allen, Thomas and Edward Post Esquires, Barristers at Law, to whom much credit is due for helping the ladies out of the windows of the carriages, the doors of which were blocked up on one side by the railings and the other side being locked. We are glad that these gentlemen have escaped with a few bruises, for had anything dangerous occurred to them it would have caused a very serious vacancy in the South Wales law circuit.

It took just over a year to extend the line westward to Haverfordwest, crossing the Towy at Carmarthen by way of an iron bridge, hinged to allow it to be raised for the passage of ships. On Wednesday the 28th of December, 1853, the people of Pembrokeshire celebrated in grand style the arrival of the first, ceremonial train. Several hundred people travelled on the train, which left Swansea at 8.45 a.m. and arrived in Haverfordwest at 12.30 p.m., to be met by civic dignitaries with a formal address of welcome. A huge procession followed the bands of the 1st Royals, the Castlemartin Yeomanry Cavalry and the Pembroke Dockyard Battalion to a 'Public Breakfast'. A public holiday was declared and after a spectacular firework display from the railway embankment, the celebrations were rounded off by a Grand Ball in the railway terminus building. Exhausted by the night-long dancing to Lawrence's Quadrille Band, the revellers returned eastwards on their special train, calculating no doubt that the all-in charge from Swansea of twelve shillings and sixpence [62½p] and seven shillings and sixpence [37½p] for the ladies had been well worthwhile.

This new-found freedom of the ordinary man to explore beyond walking distance is exemplified in just two contemporary accounts of a new phenomenon which came with the railway . . . the works outing:

Excursion of employees: On Monday last [19th July, 1869] the workmen and their families employed at the Carmarthen Tinworks had their fourth annual excursion, Tenby being selected for the day's enjoyment. Messrs. Thomas, Lester & Co., the proprietors of these works, who are ever-ready to promote good fellowship between employers and employed, entered heartily into the movement and made arrangements with the Whitland and Tenby Railway Company to run an excursion train at a nominal rate, so as to allow even the most humble in their works to afford for themselves the treat, the day being liberally granted them.

At nine o'clock about five hundred people, including about three hundred from the works, started from Carmarthen Station and made their first trip to the "Brighton of Wales" without break of gauge in about an hour and a quarter. Arriving at their destination the parties dispersed for their holiday and on their rearrival at the station at half past seven in the evening, it was gratifying to observe that not one per cent betrayed the trust imposed in them by indulging too free in inebriating liquors. This reflects much credit on the men, and also on Messrs. Owen, Jones and Jarrett, under whose immediate supervision they work, while to Messrs. Thomas, Lester & Co. it must be most satisfactory to know that their labourers are worthy of their hire.

Workmen's treat: On Monday last [20th September, 1875] the officers, workmen and other employees engaged by Messrs. Norton Brothers, Brewers, at their brewery and other works in Carmarthen, received from their employers the usual annual treat, of which their wives &c. partook. On this occasion the workmen went on an excursion to Milford, the great attraction thither being to see the Great Eastern,[3] which is lying at the docks for the purpose of being repaired and redecorated. The party number sixty-seven, and it is gratifying to be able to state that not a single case of misconduct or intemperance occurred during the trip.

The significance of the comments on the sobriety of these two events will not be lost on those acquainted with the valiant efforts of the temperance campaigners at the time, in a Carmarthen dubbed by an influential weekly newspaper "the town possessed of the most drunken inhabitants in Wales".[4]

A great crowd-pulling event of July, 1862, provided further dramatic evidence of the way in which the railway had revolutionised the way of life of ordinary people. Carmarthen's Grand Musical Eisteddfod was held in a large shed erected for the purpose in the Market Place:

. . . fitted up in a most complete manner so as to accommodate several thousands and handsomely and tastefully decorated with appropriate motifs and festoons of evergreens and shrubs. The decorations were done under the superintendence of the Misses Goode of Llanllwch, assisted by some other ladies, who devoted the whole of the previous days in the week to their good work.

The Eisteddfod opened with a grand concert in the King Street Assembly Rooms on the night before the main event, and on the big day:

> Early in the morning, trains brought into the town a great number of visitors, and when the gates of the market were opened at ten o'clock the place in a short time was comfortably filled, even before the excursion trains which were expected any moment had arrived. About twelve o'clock the excursionists made their appearance to the number of three thousand. These filled up every available space in the shed and avenues adjoining, so that by midday there could not have been less than five to six thousand persons present.

These railway excursions had opened up a new world to ordinary people, and 1862 saw trips from Carmarthen to such events as Epsom Races, the 'Great Cattle Show' at Battersea, London, and the Handel Festival at the Crystal Palace, at fares of twenty-seven shillings [£1.35] 1st class and seventeen shillings [85p] in a lower class "covered carriage".

Such was the impact of the almost overnight transition from stagecoach to rail travel that a mere ten years after the railway arrived at Carmarthen, under the heading 'Coach Accident', the *Carmarthen Journal* could reflect that:

> In these go-ahead of railways and steam power, a heading like the one annexed to this paragraph seems to carry us back an age, to a time when neither street nor underground railways were dreamed or thought of,[5] to the time of burly stage-coachmen and gaily attired guards, whose shrill horns waked the echoes of many silent spots and the slumbers of many a somnolent gatekeeper, when the maximum speed in travelling was obtainable only in one of those conveyances 'licensed to carry four inside and eight out.' The 'Good old Coaching Days' as they are wont to be designated by those who revel in a recollection of mail coach journeys, are well-nigh reckoned as things of the past, few of those vehicles still climbing our hills and careering gaily through our valleys. But even they are not of the old type, partaking rather of the natures of the modern omnibus than the old mail coach.

But what were the more immediate effects of the arrival of the Railway Age in Carmarthen? Let the *Carmarthen Journal* speak again:

> Increase of Traffic: Since the Autumn of last year [1852] when

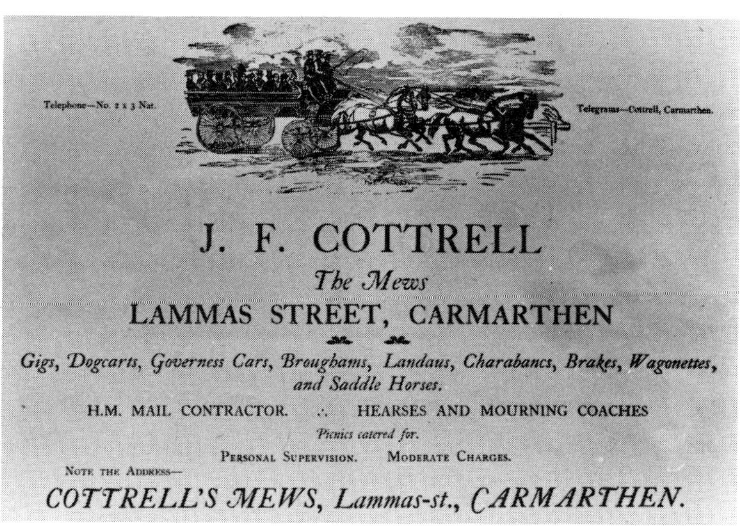


A "modern omnibus": an advertisement from the end of the 19th century. *(Mrs. Anne Davies, Trevaughan).*

the railway was opened to Carmarthen, the traffic in this district has increased in a most remarkable manner, far beyond what was anticipated, even by those who expected the most. In this town it is quadruple what it was twelve months ago and at that time there was an increase on the preceding year.

The coaches and omnibusses are crowded, over-laden, every day, and many parties are often unable to find room on them. The bustle in the streets is very much more than was formerly the case. Trade is now as active here as in English towns. This is not altogether attributable to the general prosperity, for on many occasions when trade was brisk in England it was not so here. We rather think it is due to the facility of transit afforded by the Railway. Our markets on Saturday are fully supplied and quickly cleared at good prices. Farmers sell their corn and cattle readily at prices regulated by the English markets. These things are in abundance sent off by rail and the vendors, with the ready money paid for their commodities, buy many luxuries as well as the necessaries of life with the tradespeople of the town.

Signs of continued prosperity are everywhere visible.

Of course, much more was to happen over the rest of the century in terms of the spread of the railway network, the development of its engines and rolling stock, and the speed and cheapness of its services, in what was to be the Golden Age of the railways. And it would happen quickly. Carmarthen would soon become a most important junction, for lines spreading in all directions into the hitherto remote hinterland, and within a very few years the Ganymede, the Pearl and the Caliban would look positively prehistoric when compared with their sleek successors. But none of this would have anything like the impact of the arrival in Carmarthen on that sunny September day in 1852 of that very first passenger train.

It was an event without parallel in the history of the old town. What the Ganymede, the Pearl and the Caliban had brought with them to Carmarthen was something far more precious than their happy passengers, their band of music and their beaming dignitaries. They had brought the world to Carmarthen's door.

Thus 'The Mighty Power of Steam'.

## NOTES

[1] It may be that not a little of their enthusiasm arose from the knowledge that the railway navvies' shanty-town was by then ten miles away, in Carmarthen!

[2] To-day, 130 years later, the same journeys take—Llanelli 22 mins.; Swansea 49 mins.; Cardiff 1 hour 47 mins.; and London between 3 hours 40 mins. and 4 hours.

[3] Isambard Kingdom Brunel's great, but unsuccessful, transatlantic steamship, built in 1858. By the time of this outing (1875) the 18,915 ton giant had been converted into a cable layer.

[4] See *A Shilling for Carmarthen,* Chapter 10—'An Army Vast, The Temperance Host'.

[5] The first London underground railway had been opened just one month before this was written—on the 10th of January, 1863.

An old coaching inn enters the 20th century: The Ivy Bush, with its own motor omnibus for taking patrons to and from the railway station.
*(Theo Rogers)*.

# Ships

''Rivers are roads which move, and which carry us whither we desire to go''.

Pascal (1670)

# SHIPS

Standing on Carmarthen's crumbling quay to-day and looking along a neglected riverside, beyond the old railway swing bridge and to the wooded hillsides that enfold the winding River Towy on its ten mile journey to the sea, it is hard to imagine that that river was once Carmarthen's artery—its main highway to the outside world over centuries that stretch back almost beyond history. It is hard to imagine that as the nineteenth century dawned it saw a forest of masts and rigging along the quay wall and on the river; it saw ships in building on the banks below the quay; it saw sixty Carmarthen-registered vessels; it saw a busy Customs House on the quay and it saw a river alive with four hundred coracles and with innumerable small boats carrying passengers and goods to and from Llanstephan and Ferryside at the river's mouth.

Here cannon boomed from a dozen ships, dressed overall to salute Nelson's victory at Trafalgar, and here the Carmarthen Mob thrashed the dreaded and hitherto invincible Press-gang and drove them from the town—never to return—in a unique display of strength. One night in 1803, two years before Trafalgar, the 'Polly' tender of a man o' war standing in Carmarthen Bay, came up river under muffled oars and landed the dreaded Press-gang to scour the streets and to press men for service in the King's wartime navy. The town bell rang and Mayor Paxton was obliged to swear in a large number of special constables to save the sailors from being lynched. They retreated down river pursued by the curses and missiles of the mob, and with no recruits to show for their visit.[1] And here, along this quay, the cavalry clattered with sabres drawn, to the aid of town magistrates trying to prevent the ransacking of food cargoes by starving hundreds; here stood a vast and cheering crowd to welcome the 'Frolic' and the flotilla of small boats that had gone down river to greet this first steamship ever to come to Carmarthen Quay. From here, paddle steamers like the 'Prince of Wales', the 'Nelson' and the 'Talbot', packed to their rails with happy, cheering "excursionists", thrashed and hooted their way down river bound for the seaside resorts of Devon and Pembrokeshire, waved off by the inevitable crowds on the quay and the river banks. And here, on the river and its banks, successive generations of Carmarthen people watched the firework displays, the regattas and the coracle races, events that made the river rival Guildhall Square as the focal point of old Carmarthen's unparalleled capacity for celebration.

It was all there, on that short stretch of river, a river now deserted, and separated from the town it once served so well.[2]

At the beginning of the nineteenth century, when Carmarthen was comparatively isolated on its landward side, it was to the River Towy and to the sea that she looked for her trade; down from the busy markets, beyond the decaying but still majestic castle gateway, through narrow Bridge Street and

"Down from the busy markets, through narrow Quay Street, to the short, cargo-stacked quay." *(National Library of Wales).*

Quay Street, where steep crowded terraces and winding steps spilled past numerous alehouses down to the quay. This short, cargo-stacked quay was the berth for vessels from as far away as the Americas and for those of a busy coastal trade, from Tenby, Devon, Bristol, London, Ireland and Scotland. White-sailed ships glided around the bends of the winding river, down the broad green valley to the Bristol Channel, carrying timber, bark, marble, slate, bricks, lead ore, butter, cheese, eggs, oats, barley, wheat, malt and many other cargoes. And imports, too, travelled that river, in ships like Captain Ovens's 'Ceres', bringing salt from Gloucester, Captain Lewis's 'Expedition' laden with Devonshire earthenware from Bideford, Captain Roberts's 'Providence' with iron from Newport, and regular coal ships like the 'Friendship' with Captain Hickson, the 'Mary Anne' with Captain Morgan and the 'Jane' with Captain Leonard, sailing up from Llanelli.

There was keen competition for the merchants' charters between ships' masters like Captain Patrick, master of the brig 'Industry', who made a "remarkably fast" Atlantic passage from Lewis Town in Nova Scotia to Carmarthen laden with fir timber. He reported to Mr. Morgan Lewis, the Carmarthen merchant, within twenty-nine days of setting sail. And the owners of the 'Carmarthen Packet' and her master David Jones bid fair to capture a lucrative share of the coastal trade when:

> . . . having come down channel [from Bristol] in company with eighty vessels of different descriptions she outsailed them all, and is considered the fastest sailing vessel that ever arrived at our quay, and will be kept on the Bristol trade.

The more extensive facilities which this growing trade demanded were provided (in 1808 and 1809) by a lengthening of the quay from the Jolly Tar Inn[3] to the town bridge, and by the construction of another dock near the Pothouse, to join Bedford's yard in the building of Carmarthen's own sloops and brigs—some as large as three hundred tons—of which some sixty were registered at the port.

A launching was guaranteed to bring out the crowds, and was always a cause for feasting and celebration, as when:

> On Wednesday eve, the 25th of September, 1805 a beautiful

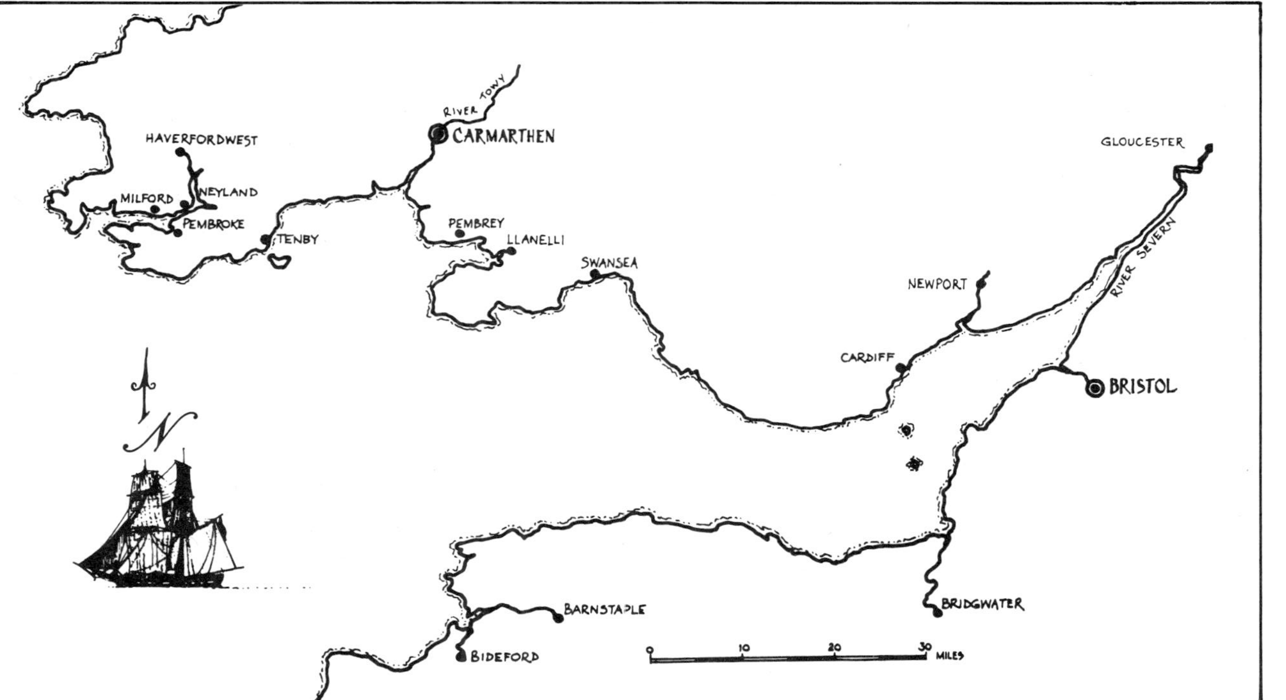


The Bristol Channel. *(Pat Molloy).*

**NEW TRADER**

BETWEEN

**CARMARTHEN AND BRISTOL.**

THE new Smack, ELIZABETH, is trading regularly between Carmarthen and Bristol, and will leave the latter place positively in six days from the commencement of taking in Goods.

Gentlemen and Trades-men may depend upon their Goods being quickly conveyed to and from Bristol, as the *Elizabeth* is a remarkably fast sailing Vessel, and well adapted for the Trade.

For further particulars apply to the Captain on Board; to Mr. James Boswell, No. 11, Welsh Back, Bristol; at the Duke of Buckingham, Carmarthen; or to the Carmarthen Agent, John Jenkins.

☞ No charge whatever for warehousing Goods at Carmarthen will be made.

By sailing ship: The 'Elizabeth' loads at Bristol for Carmarthen. *(Carmarthen Journal).*

brig was launched at Carmarthen by Mr. Hughes, a merchant of the town, named 'Mary Anne' after his youngest daughter. At seven o'clock she went down and took to the water in majestic style, amidst the acclamation of an immense crowd of spectators. Mr. Hughes, with about seventy or eighty of his friends, afterwards sat down to an elegant supper, with every delicacy the season could afford. A number of patriotic songs and toasts enlivened the remainder of the night, when the company retired, highly delighted with the liberality and attention of their benevolent host. (Cambrian)

And again, eight months later:

A fine, ready-rigged brig was on Monday evening last, the 5th of May, 1806, launched at Carmarthen. She is called the 'Priscilla' in honour of Mrs. Rees, the lady of Mr. Rees, Merchant, the principal owner. The men scarcely had time to strike off one bridle when she glided into the water carrying the other bridle away in a most majestic style. The evening being favourable, there was an immense assemblage of persons present at the ceremony. On the following night, the owners entertained a select party of eight friends with a cold supper, consisting of every delicacy in season, and the glass circulated freely until a late hour. (Cambrian)

Many Carmarthen men followed the hard trade of the sea, and many were taken by that merciless element. Nineteenth century records abound with stories of shipwrecks on the treacherous sands of Carmarthen Bay, most of them through the violence of storms, but not a few through the taking of false bearings from fires lit on the shores of the Burry Estuary by the

19th century shipwrecks in Carmarthen Bay. *(Pat Molloy).*

Dynion y Bwyelli Bach—the men of the little axes—a name which still attaches to the people of that locality. It was they, some said, who had removed recently-placed buoys, an impediment to their nefarious wrecking and plundering. Whether or not a stranding was engineered by the wreckers, the news of it would spread like wild-fire and the race would be on; people from miles around swarmed to the sea shore on foot and with pack-horses and carts to strip the wreck, while the authorities fought an often losing battle to stop them. There being no effective police, it fell to the army to do the job, as when it was ordered that:

> The Officers, Non-Commissioned Officers and Drummers [of The Royal Carmarthenshire Militia] will assemble on the Parade, Carmarthen, as soon as possible in order to march to the Ferry [Ferryside] to protect a wreck now on the Cefn Sidan, the men to be provided with ten rounds of ball cartridges and a good flint. The Officers will appear in their undress coats and cocked hats.[4]

The Dynion y Bwyelli Bach were still at it as late as 1886 when five of them were prosecuted for plundering the wreck of the four-master 'Teviotdale' and robbing the bodies washed up on Cefn Sidan sands. Eighteen lives had been lost from the ship in a dreadful storm.[5]

In the early years of the century, there were not only the storms and the wreckers to contend with. There were the French, with whom we were at war. Captain George of Carmarthen, with two of his ship's mates and two boys, was taken from his brig 'Flora' while anchored about a mile off Margate in Kent. Thanks to the efforts of the crews of nearby ships, the French were prevented from cutting the anchor and capturing the ship, but they carried their prisoners back to France. The Carmarthen smack 'Thetis' was even more unlucky. With her master, Joseph Harries, she was captured complete with crew and cargo of valuable Carmarthen tinplate, and taken into Calais.

In the 1820s steamships first appeared in the Bristol Channel, and it became quicker to get to Bristol by taking the road west, to Pembrokeshire. In May, 1830, the public were:

> . . . most respectfully informed that the Cambrian light post coach will commence running between Carmarthen and Tenby on

The 'Glamorgan', one of the first steamships on the Bristol Channel, entered service in 1823. *(Swansea Maritime and Industrial Museum).*

> Tuesday the 23rd of May, 1830, and will continue to run from the Boar's Head Inn, Carmarthen, on Tuesday, Thursday and Saturday mornings at ten o'clock, to the Coburg Hotel, Tenby, and from thence to Carmarthen on Monday, Wednesday and Friday at eleven o'clock in the forenoon. The coach will meet the Glamorgan, Bristol and Tenby steam packets [at Tenby] and the Hereford, Worcester and London coaches [at Carmarthen].

Six months later, Carmarthen entered the age of the steamship for the first time in her own right, when the General Steam Packet Company of Bristol announced that they were introducing to the Carmarthen trade a fine new paddle steamer of nearly a hundred horse power, capable of carrying ". . . upwards of a hundred tons of goods, with excellent accommodations for every description of livestock". The steamer 'Frolic', commanded by Captain Jenkins, would carry passengers in every possible comfort, the proprietors being ". . . anxious that the regularity, cleanliness and comfort of the vessel should give general satisfaction", and announcing that "The cabins for the ladies and gentlemen are distinct and convenient and the dining room communicates with both. A female steward attends the ladies' cabins."

The service would run alternately between Bristol and Carmarthen, and Bristol and Haverfordwest, on the latter passage calling at Milford and Pembroke, and on both ". . . calling off Tenby where practicable to land and receive passengers". As for the cost of this fast and comfortable mode of travel, one could have a cabin for twenty-one shillings [£1.05][6] with a steward's fee of two-shillings [10 pence], or travel steerage at ten shillings and sixpence [52½ pence], while taking one's horse at twenty-five shillings [£1.25], one's four-wheeled carriage for two pounds, or a two-wheeled one for twenty-five shillings [£1.25].

The 'Frolic's' first arrival in Carmarthen, on the 24th of November, 1830, brought out the whole town. It was reported that:

> Her reception was extremely flattering; an immense concourse of the inhabitants went some miles down the river in a fleet of boats to greet her arrival, and if we may take public feeling running strongly in her favour to be a pressage there can be little doubt of her ultimate success. The 'Frolic' is a very fine vessel. Her accommodations are of superior character, and for speed, power and tonnage she is not equalled in any port in the Principality. She accomplished the voyage between Bristol and Tenby in ten hours and a half, and out-distanced five packets that left Bristol at the same time, including the 'Lee', the 'Palmerston', and the 'Bristol'.

But the 'Frolic' was a doomed ship, and the inhabitants of the port of Carmarthen were once again to be reminded of the fearsome power of the sea and of the treachery of the Bristol Channel. Only four months after her enthusiastic reception on the Towy she foundered:

> . . . on her passage from Haverfordwest to Bristol during the tempestuous night of Wednesday 16th, or early on Thursday morning, 17th March, 1831. The scene of this distressing event was the Naas Sands on the Glamorganshire coast, within a short distance of Cowbridge. It is supposed that the accident happened between three and four o'clock in the morning and that the vessel went to pieces very shortly after she struck. She was commanded by Captain Jenkins and had on board an experienced channel pilot

*Bristol, Ilfracombe, and Tenby*

**STEAM-PACKET**

**GLAMORGAN.**

THE Public are respectfully informed, That the GLAMORGAN will commence sailing on MONDAY, the 26th of APRIL, leaving BRISTOL for ILFRACOMBE, at half past 8 o'clock Morning, & returning from ILFRACOMBE on Tuesday at 10 o'clock Morning.

She will sail from BRISTOL for TENBY on Thursday, 29th April, at 10 o'clock Morning, and return from Tenby on Saturday, 1st May, at 10 o'clock Morning; and will continue to sail between the above places on the same days until the end of May, after which she will sail TWICE a week to Ilfracombe, and ONCE a week to Tenby.

Bills, with the hours of sailing, &c. are issued Monthly, and may be obtained in LONDON of Mr. Chaplin, Spread Eagle Inn, Gracechurch Street; at the Spread Eagle Office, Piccadilly; and at Osborne's Hotels, Adelphi; in ILFRACOMBE of Mr. Martin, Britannia Hotel; in TENBY of Mr. George Hughes, Cobourg Hotel; and with every other information by applying (if by letter, post paid) to

JOHN JONES, Agent,
Bristol Steam-Packet Offices,
Rownham Wharf, Hotwells, and
St. Stephen's Avenue, Bristol.

April, 1830.

The 'Glamorgan' could be met at Tenby by a stage coach connection from Carmarthen.

*(Carmarthen Journal).*

*Steam Packet Communication*

BETWEEN

**BRISTOL**

AND

**CARMARTHEN,**

AND

***BRISTOL***

AND

**HAVERFORDWEST,**

AND PLACES ADJACENT.

THE STEAM PACKET, *Frolic*, Edward Jenkins, R.N., Commander, is intended to sail between Bristol and Carmarthen, calling off Tenby, when practicable, to land and receive Passengers, as under; and between Bristol and Haverfordwest, calling off Tenby, when practicable, to land and receive Passengers, and taking in Goods for Milford and Pembroke Dock, at Shippers' Risk, as under.

*From Bristol to Carmarthen.*
Friday, Jan. 14 ... 6 Morn. | Friday, Jan. 28... 6 Morn.

*From Carmarthen to Bristol.*
Tuesday, Jan. 18.. 7 Morn. | Monday, Jan. 31.. 7 Morn.

*From Bristol to Haverfordwest.*
Saturday, Jan. 8.. 1 Aftern. | Thursday, Jan. 20. 10 Morn.

*From Haverfordwest to Bristol*
Tuesday, Jan. 11..3 Aftern. | Monday, Jan. 24..12 Noon.

Cabin, 21s. Steward's Fee, 2s.; Steerage, 10s. 6d.; Horse, 25s.; Four-wheel Carriage, £2; Two-wheel ditto, 25s.; Dog, 3s.

The Proprietors are anxious that the regularity, cleanliness, and comfort of the vessel shall give general satisfaction.

The Cabins for the Ladies and Gentlemen are distinct and convenient; the Dining Room communicates with both.—A Female Steward attends the Ladies' Cabin.

The *Frolic* is a new Vessel of nearly 100 Horses Power, will carry upwards of 100 tons of Goods, with excellent accommodations for every description of Live Stock.

For particulars, enquire at the General Steam Packet Office, 1, Quay, Bristol; of Mr. Gibbon, Haverfordwest; or of Mr. Walter Harris, Milford.

☞ All Goods, Packages, and Parcels, addressed as above, or to Mr. Geo. Francis, at the Packet House, (Pelican Inn,) Carmarthen, will be forwarded to all parts, without delay, where Passengers and others will find every accommodation, and obtain all necessary information respecting the *Frolic* and the other Steamer that is to sail between Carmarthen and Bristol.

**NOTICE.**—The Proprietors of the above Steam Packet will not be accountable for any Cabin Passenger's Luggage, (if lost or damaged,) above the value of £5; nor for any Deck Passenger's Luggage, (if lost or damaged,) above the value of 20s. unless in each case entered as such, and freight in proportion paid for the same, at the time of delivery, nor will they be answerable for any other parcel above the value of 40s. (if lost or damaged,) unless entered as such, and freight in proportion paid for the same, at the time of delivery.—December, 1830.

*Carmarthen and Tenby.*

THE Public are most respectfully informed, that an elegant and light POST-COACH, called the

**CAMBRIAN,**

Will commence running between the above-mentioned places, on Tuesday, 14th of June, and will continue during the Season.

It will start from the Boar's Head, Carmarthen, every Tuesday, Thursday, and Saturday mornings, at 10 o'clock; and from Tenby every Monday, Wednesday, and Friday mornings, at 11 o'clock.

JOHN DAVIES, Proprietor.

Carmarthen, May 27th, 1831.

The 'Cambrian' coach met steamers at Tenby.

*(Carmarthen Journal).*

"Carmarthen entered the age of the steamship for the first time in her own right in November, 1830." The 'Frolic'.

*(Carmarthen Journal).*

and a crew of thirteen men, besides a number of passengers from Haverfordwest, Milford and Tenby, of whom it is feared no correct list can be obtained, every soul having perished.

The latest accounts brought by the Bristol Mail [coach] state the number to be fifty-one, and that besides the Captain, whose body was picked up on the Friday and taken to Bristol on the Saturday, sixteen other bodies, including that of a woman with a child in her arms, and that of a young lady named Henderson of Milford, had been washed ashore. The Captain was found lashed to part of the rigging.

The first intelligence of this melancholy event was taken to Bristol on Thursday by the 'Bristol' steamer of Swansea, the Captain stating that he was impeded in his passage by floating pieces of wreck and that he saw one of the paddle-boxes on the coast and a boiler and part of the engine on the sands. The Captain, whose family resided at Haverfordwest, has left a wife who is pregnant, and nine children. The mate, who resided at Pill, a wife and five children.

The loss of the 'Frolic' was the second maritime tragedy to hit Carmarthen within a space of four months. The first was even closer to home, to one of the town's own ships, the sloop 'Hero', under one of its own captains, George Morgan. On a day in November, 1830, she was:

. . . bound from Llanelli with coals to this town, and was proceeding up the bay when a dreadful gale came on. The wind rent every sail they had, and the sea rushed fearfully over her, sweeping away every article from the deck and carrying off the hatches. The crew, seeing their perilous situation, put her before the wind to run for shore, and then proceeded up the rigging to lash themselves to the masts. At this critical moment the captain's wife, who had just left the cabin, came to join her husband and he was in the act of carrying her in his arms to the shrouds when a heavy sea struck them and took her away from his hold. Realising that human aid was inadequate to save her life, he made for the rigging and lashed himself with the crew, where they remained until the vessel stranded near Pendine.

When the tide had sufficiently receded, they came to the deck and on looking into the hold, the first object that presented itself to them was the captain's wife, a lifeless corpse. On Tuesday 23rd November, 1830, her remains were interred in Llangain Churchyard near this town.

Despite the worsening state of the river for want of proper

dredging (for which the corporation would soon be called to account by a Parliamentary Commission), the sailing ship traffic was still brisk. In and out of the port during a week in 1831 were the 'Mary', under Captain Lewis, the 'Britannia' (Captain Phillips), the 'Halcyon' (Captain Tanner), the 'Anne and Maria' (Captain Wathen), the 'Nightingale' (Captain Brooks), the 'Princess Royal' (Captain Morgan), the 'Minerva' (Captain Owen), the 'Four Brothers' (Captain Booth), the 'Peggy' (Captain Webb), the 'Mary Anne' (Captain Thomas), 'Industry' (Captain Thomas), the 'Thomas' (Captain Jones), the 'Bett and Peggy' (Captain Meyrick), the 'Farmer's Delight' (Captain Morgan), the 'Friend's Good-will' (Captain Hancock), the 'William' (Captain Paynter), the 'Providence' (Captain Shankland), the 'Acorn' (Captain Protheroe), the 'William and Anne' (Captain Phillips), the 'Hope' (Captain Cadwallader) and the 'Emerald Isle' (Captain Thomas), sailing between Carmarthen and Llanelli, Bristol, Swansea, Newport, Dublin, Waterford, Wexford, Dungarvan, Cork and Cardiff. In July, 1830, the Carmarthen Liquor Merchant, John Morgan, introduced an improved cargo connection with London when he announced that:

> The fast sailing schooner 'John Saint Barbe', Evan Davies master, now loading at Pickleherring Wharf, London, for Milford, Haverfordwest, Pembroke, Tenby, Carmarthen and places adjacent, will sail as per agreement by the owners of the 'John Saint Barbe', the 'Emerald Isle' and the 'Sarah', that each of the three vessels shall leave in rotation monthly, whether they have full cargoes or not. Shippers may therefore rely on a more speedy delivery of their goods.

And some record passages were being made, the 'Emerald Isle' referred to in that advertisement having recently broken the record from London by making the passage in *four* days!

Of course, London could be reached in *two* days by passengers travelling by coach, but the class of person who could afford to travel regularly by coach in those days may be judged by the fact that the Chief Constable of Carmarthen would have had to spend nearly two months salary on a return trip to London . . . assuming he travelled inside, which he would be wise to do, since it was not unknown for outside passengers to freeze to death on winter journeys!

Shipping was still the cheapest and most efficient means of conveying goods and passengers, so the coasting trade flourished. Sailing ships carried the bulk of the trade; ships like:

> The Fast Sailing Smack 'Milford Packet', loading goods at the Pickleherring Wharf, London, for Carmarthen and places adjacent. The regularity with which the London trade has conveyed goods to this part of the Principality has proved of immense benefit to the mercantile interest as well as to the community at large.
>
> Vessels now leave Pickleherring Wharf for the ports of South Wales every fortnight, affording a favourable opportunity to merchants and others of procuring their goods from the London markets.
>
> For further particulars apply to the Captain on board, or to Mr. T. Morgan, Spirit Merchant, Carmarthen.

And the Carmarthen shipbuilders were still very much in business, as when:

> The 'Naiad', a beautiful brig about 140 tons registered, nearly wholely rigged, was on Saturday morning [26th February, 1838] launched from the Pothouse Quay in this town and proved a very interesting sight. She has been built by Messrs. Phillips and Lewis, Timber Merchants of this town, and is to be employed on the Baltic timber trade.

But sailing ships were at the mercy of capricious winds, and Carmarthen had had no direct steamer service since the loss of the 'Frolic' in 1830, and by December, 1833, after a near-disastrous period of adverse winds, the town's merchants were showing their impatience:

> To merchants, shopkeepers and all other tradesmen of Carmarthen and its neighbourhood and the adjoining Counties of Cardigan and Pembroke. Notice is hereby given that in consequence of the very great inconvenience, loss and expense the trade has experienced in consequence of the long and continued westerly winds which have prevented the regular traders between this port and Bristol from completing their voyages from Bristol to this port for the last six weeks, and in some instances two months, the public are respectfully informed that a company of merchants

> and tradesmen is being formed for the purpose of collecting in shares of £50 each a sufficient sum for the purchase of a good and substantial steamer of sufficient strength and power to ply between Carmarthen and Bristol exclusively, and to perform the voyage in ten or twelve hours, for the transmission of passengers, goods and livestock thereto. Address, John Llewellyn, Merchant, Guildhall Square, Carmarthen.

It would take time for this enterprise to take to the water, but within six months a paddle steamer was once again plying the River Towy from the Bristol Channel, under the ownership (as was the ill-fated 'Frolic') of the Bristol General Steam Navigation Company, who advertised a steamship service between Bristol, Wales and Cornwall. The public were informed that:

> The 'County of Pembroke' of 100 horse-power, B. Matthews, Commander, is intended to perform voyages between Bristol and Carmarthen, from Cumberland Basin, on July the 3rd [1834] and after. Fares: Cabin £1.2.6d. [£1.12½p]; Deck 10s.6d. [52½p]; Children under 12 years half-price; Large four-wheeled carriage £2.12s.6d. [£2.62½p]; Small and two-wheeled carriage £1.10s.0d. [£1.50p]; Horses £1.5s.0d. [£1.25p]; Dogs 3s.0d. [15p]. Refreshments at fixed prices; a female attendant.
>
> The 'County of Pembroke' is a remarkably fast packet. It has a private cabin for ladies, a spacious dining room, and a gentlemen's sleeping cabin.
>
> She will perform the voyage in twelve or fourteen hours, weather permitting, and thus facilitate the communications between Bristol and Cardigan, Aberystwyth, Milford, Lampeter, Llandeilo &c.[7]

The 1840s were the heyday of the Port of Carmarthen, and the air of optimism in the town over its maritime future betokened an absence of any real appreciation of what lay in store with the approach of a rival form of communication. The railway was snaking its way westward from the banks of the Severn at Chepstow and was fast approaching Swansea, but in a Carmarthen where the coach was king and the paddle steamer queen, the iron road might have been a thousand miles away. In October, 1846, under the heading 'Trade of the Port', the *Carmarthen Journal* was:

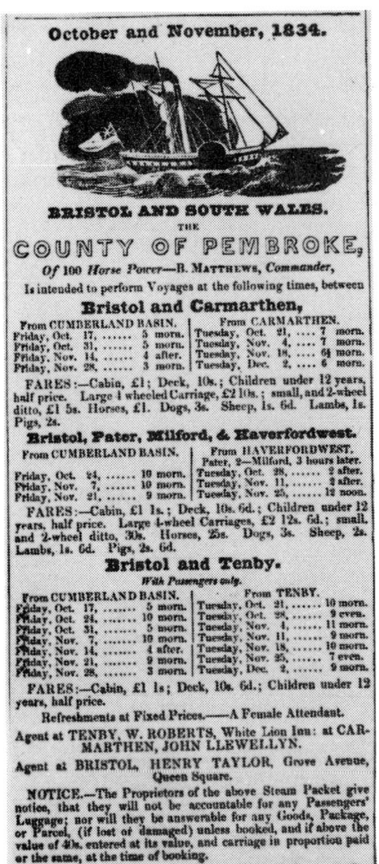

October and November, 1834.

BRISTOL AND SOUTH WALES.

THE

COUNTY OF PEMBROKE,

*Of* 100 *Horse Power*—B. MATTHEWS, *Commander*,

Is intended to perform Voyages at the following times, between

**Bristol and Carmarthen,**

| From CUMBERLAND BASIN. | From CARMARTHEN. |
|---|---|
| Friday, Oct. 17, ...... 5 morn. | Tuesday, Oct. 21, .... 7 morn. |
| Friday, Oct. 31, ...... 5 morn. | Tuesday, Nov. 4, .... 7 morn. |
| Friday, Nov. 14, ...... 4 after. | Tuesday, Nov. 18, .... 6½ morn. |
| Friday, Nov. 28, ...... 3 morn. | Tuesday, Dec. 2, .... 6 morn. |

FARES:—Cabin, £1; Deck, 10s.; Children under 12 years, half price. Large 4 wheeled Carriage, £2 10s.; small, and 2-wheel ditto, £1 5s. Horses, £1. Dogs, 3s. Sheep, 1s. 6d. Lambs, 1s. Pigs, 2s.

**Bristol, Pater, Milford, & Haverfordwest.**

| From CUMBERLAND BASIN. | From HAVERFORDWEST. Pater, 2—Milford, 3 hours later. |
|---|---|
| Friday, Oct. 24, ...... 10 morn. | Tuesday, Oct. 28, ...... 2 after. |
| Friday, Nov. 7, ...... 10 morn. | Tuesday, Nov. 11, ...... 2 after. |
| Friday, Nov. 21, ...... 9 morn. | Tuesday, Nov. 25, ...... 12 noon. |

FARES:—Cabin, £1 1s.; Deck, 10s. 6d.; Children under 12 years, half price. Large 4-wheel Carriages, £2 12s. 6d.; small, and 2-wheel ditto, 30s. Horses, 25s. Dogs, 3s. Sheep, 2s. Lambs, 1s. 6d. Pigs, 2s. 6d.

**Bristol and Tenby.**

*With Passengers only.*

| From CUMBERLAND BASIN. | From TENBY. |
|---|---|
| Friday, Oct. 17, ...... 5 morn. | Tuesday, Oct. 21, ...... 10 morn. |
| Friday, Oct. 24, ...... 10 morn. | Tuesday, Oct. 28, ...... 9 even. |
| Friday, Oct. 31, ...... 5 morn. | Tuesday, Nov. 4, ...... 11 morn. |
| Friday, Nov. 7, ...... 10 morn. | Tuesday, Nov. 11, ...... 9 morn. |
| Friday, Nov. 14, ...... 4 after. | Tuesday, Nov. 18, ...... 10 morn. |
| Friday, Nov. 21, ...... 9 morn. | Tuesday, Nov. 25, ...... 7 even. |
| Friday, Nov. 28, ...... 3 morn. | Tuesday, Dec. 2, ...... 9 morn. |

FARES:—Cabin, £1 1s; Deck, 10s. 6d.; Children under 12 years, half price.

Refreshments at Fixed Prices.——A Female Attendant.

Agent at TENBY, W. ROBERTS, White Lion Inn: at CARMARTHEN, JOHN LLEWELLYN.

Agent at BRISTOL, HENRY TAYLOR, Grove Avenue, Queen Square.

NOTICE.—The Proprietors of the above Steam Packet give notice, that they will not be accountable for any Passengers' Luggage; nor will they be answerable for any Goods, Package, or Parcel, (if lost or damaged) unless booked, and if above the value of 40s. entered at its value, and carriage in proportion paid or the same, at the time of booking.

The 'County of Pembroke' resumes Carmarthen's steamer connection with Bristol.
*(Carmarthen Journal).*

> . . . glad to find that the trade of the port is steadily increasing, to judge by the large importation of goods that arrive every week. The barge of the 'Phoenix' steamer, which until lately was found sufficient to convey the freights of the 'Phoenix' up to the Quay [from its anchorage at Blackpool, two miles down river] is to be considerably enlarged in consequence of the increasing cargoes. The sailing vessels also continue to arrive as regularly as the weather will permit, well stocked with goods.

Not only were passenger and freight services booming, but the river also made a large contribution to the improvement of the lives of the ordinary people of the town through the medium of cheap excursions, works outings and, for the first time, outings for the children of the town.

Despite the criticism, so easily levelled with the benefit of a century's hindsight, that the motives behind the Charity Schools and the (older) Sunday Schools were less than altruistic and that they displayed "too great an anxiety to keep the young scholars in their appointed sphere of life and train up a subservient generation",[8] their contribution to the emancipation of the labouring class is self-evident. It has been calculated that by the 1840s some one and a half million children were receiving religious instruction and some elementary secular education at Sunday Schools in Britain, and who can criticise an institution that could bring to poor children an experience like that of the scholars of Saint David's Church Sunday School, who, in August, 1847, were taken on their annual excursion to:

> . . . that favourite and fashionable watering place, the Ferryside. The weather being delightfully fine, a most pleasant day was anticipated, nor were these anticipations in the slightest degree disappointed.
>
> Some time before seven o'clock, the scholars, all neatly clad in their holiday apparel, made their appearance on the Quay, the place of embarkation, to take their stations in the paddle steamer 'William', which was to convey them, accompanied by their teachers, to their destination. A little before eight o'clock the steamer was released from her moorings and glided along the smooth Towy, with two boats in her wake filled with the male pupils, there not being accommodation in the steamer for the number of the children being so very great.
>
> On their way down, the various objects of interest were pointed out to the children by their teachers and some school hymns were sung, which very much enhanced the pleasure of the trip. On arriving at the Ferryside, all were safely disembarked and the children then set about enjoying themselves in different methods, the boys playing cricket and other games, and the girls gathering shells and devoting their time in such other ways as were most agreeable to them.
>
> The teachers, soon after landing, partook of an elegant lunch, after which the children were formed into procession and marched towards the seashore, and having gone nearly as far as St. Ishmael's Church they returned and arranged themselves on the rocks where having raised their tuneful voices in praise of 'Him who is the Author and Giver of all good things', the Rev. D. A. Williams, the Minister of Saint David's, addressed the children,

pointing out to them the advantages they enjoyed and the use they should make of the instruction afforded to them, exhorting them to be diligent in their studies, to be attentive and submissive to their teachers, and kind and loving to each other. Hundreds of children gathered on the rocks and on the sands in picturesque groups, all listening with the most breathless attention to the admonitions of their beloved pastor, the sea rolling along, smooth and placid as the unruffled lake, the village churches with their ivy, silent towers rising in pleasing contrast to the busy hum that surrounded them, vessels looming in the distance, beating to and fro, while in front rose Llanstephan Castle with its ruined but still majestic towers.

The children, about five hundred in number, were then reformed into procession and then walked through the village. On their return they were plentifully regaled with tea and plum cake, and at six o'clock all had again embarked, and soon after safely arrived at Carmarthen Quay, just at the time when 'Sol illumines the western sky and evening Zephyrs softly sigh'.

The Quay, the embankments and all available places were crowded with the inhabitants, who came to witness the disembarkation and who were much gratified with the scene, heightened by the beautiful silvery tones of the children once more joining in praise to their Almighty Maker.

It may well be that "To teach the peasant to read, and to put the Welsh Bible into his hands were the motives of those who established popular education throughout the length and breadth of Wales",[9] but the effect was to bring an enlightenment and literacy previously unknown to such children as these, while more and more of their elders were influenced by sermons preached in the new chapels, many of which were built or rebuilt in Carmarthen in the middle years of the nineteenth century. Seldom were such powerful seeds sown.

But there were smugglers as well as Sunday School teachers on the Towy and the customs officers stationed in the Custom House on the Island Wharf were ever vigilant. In December, 1836, for instance, before the magistrates at the Guildhall:

Mr. Thomas Rogers, Principal Coast Surveyor of the Customs in this Port, appeared to make a charge against James Hughes, the mate of the bark 'Shelmalere', unloading in the River Towy near Coed, for attempting to run on shore a bag of tobacco on which the duty had not been paid, and against Stephen Hicks for receiving the same. They were committed to prison until the instructions of the Board of Customs should be received.

One they missed, though, was a noted smuggler about whom they had had a tip-off. The customs men laid an ambush at Johnstown, close to the Royal Oak toll-gate, and pounced when the smuggler drove by with his cart-load of smuggled spirits. They could not have laid their ambush very well, or they would have been better prepared for what happened; their quarry put his horse to the gallop and flew up the hill, past Picton's Monument, driving furiously through the town and over the bridge. He outdistanced the customs men before Llangunnor (just beyond the bridge) and, so it was said, delivered his casks of spirits safely at Llanarthne. Brandy for the Parson?

A regular spirit-smuggler, this character kept his casks under the floor of his pigsty, and on one occasion during a raid on his home by customs officers he kept them at bay with a red-hot poker while his son stove in the heads of the casks and poured out the spirits. In his last smuggling operation he was intercepted in a creek near Pembroke Town by the Revenue Cutter, and he escaped by jumping from his boat . . . only to drown.

The river was booming in the 1840s; it was still Carmarthen's main highway, but the town council, apathetic as ever in the discharge of its responsibilities towards the condition and navigability of the river,[10] was already making its own contribution to the coming decline. The necessity for larger steamers like the 'Phoenix' to discharge two miles down river from the quay arose from the fact that:

> The shameful state of our river, often a matter of comment, still remains the same [in 1847]; indeed it is getting worse. This week a vessel called the 'Bodallog' of Aberystwyth, laden with grain for Tenby, owing to the want of skill on the part of her pilot grounded on Red Cliff Ford, and on the tide ebbing the vessel broke her back and she filled with water. Her cargo of barley was worth at least £600 and belonged to Mr. Waters, and it is deteriorating to the amount of at least half its value.
>
> How long will this almost criminal apathy continue to exist on the part of the local authorities?

Despite the worst that the town council could do, though, trade was good, as the Bristol Steam Navigation Company plied its trade up and down the Bristol Channel with the paddle

The 'Juverna' at Bristol, loading for Tenby and Cork.
*(Grahame Farr. West Country Passenger Steamers).*

steamers 'Talbot' and 'Phoenix' up the Towy to Carmarthen, and their larger paddlers, the 'Shamrock', the 'Iverna', the 'Sabrina', the 'Victory' and the 'Osprey' to Dublin, Waterford, Cork, Milford, Haverfordwest and Tenby. In 1848 nothing could compare with their fares and their facilities, and there was an even greater attraction as the company announced:

> Great Reduction in Freight and Fares: The celebrated splendid steamer 'Talbot', 140 horse power, Edward Lewis Morgan, Commander. This beautiful vessel, proved to be the most rapid in the Bristol Channel, will ply weekly between Bristol and Carmarthen touching at Tenby, the up and down passage) during the month of July.
>
> This vessel is elegantly fitted up for the comfort and convenience of passengers.
>
> Bristol to Tenby and Carmarthen: Fares—Cabin, twelve shillings and sixpence [62½p]; Children under twelve, six shillings [30p]; Servants, seven shillings and sixpence [37½p]; Forecabin, five shillings [25p]; Children under twelve, four shillings [20p].
>
> Carmarthen to and from Tenby: Fares—Cabin, three shillings [15p]; Forecabin, two shillings [10p].
>
> Refreshments may be had on board at moderate charges.

If the 'Talbot' was rapid, the 'Phoenix' was a record-breaker. In March, 1849:

> This gallant vessel, which has so often rode triumphantly through the severest storms, arrived in our river on Monday last [the 5th], being her first voyage after her recent outfit and extensive repairs. By the alterations in her machinery, her speed is now greatly increased, and on Monday she made one of the shortest passages on record, having steamed from Cumberland Basin [Bristol] to her station at Black Pool on the Towy in the incredibly short time of eight hours and twenty minutes, in the teeth of a heavy headwind.
>
> We are informed that this is the quickest passage ever made.

For all the glamour of the steamships, though, it was the sailing ships that still carried the bulk of the port's trade, and as an army of labourers hacked and shovelled their way along the route of the new railway on the river bank at Ferryside, they saw their proud, white-sailed competitors gliding silently past, unknowing victims of the iron shaft driving towards the heart of their Carmarthen berth. They saw Captain Phillips's 'Britannia' from Bristol, Captain Cobley's 'Liver' from Bridgwater, Captain Davies's 'Gloucester Packet' and Captain Washbourne's 'Elizabeth' come down the River Severn from Gloucester, Captain Rees's 'Good Hope' and Captain Francis's 'Claudia' from Caernarfon, Captain Daniels's 'Bee' from Cardigan, Captain Stephens's 'Wave' from Newport, Captain Stephens's 'Jane' and Captain Thomas's 'Dolphin' from Llanelli, Captain Hancock's 'John and Mary', Captain Bevan's 'Providence', Captain Rees's 'Friends' and Captain Griffiths's 'Speedwell' from Pembrey—carrying flour, slates, flagstones, stone, coal, firebricks and all manner of cargo to and from the town, cargoes that in years to come would be hauled by noisy, smoky, iron monsters alongside that same waterway.

The railway arrived in Carmarthen in 1852 to great acclaim, and though it posed a long-term threat to the shipping trade, there would be room for the steamships to both compete and collaborate with it for some time to come. Filling the gap which would exist before the line could reach Pembrokeshire, the Bristol Steam Navigation Company's Paddle Steamer 'Usk' plied between Pembrey and Tenby, linking with the London trains at Pembrey. And the company's continued confidence in the future of Carmarthen as a port was indicated by their announcement of the building of:

> A Splendid New Iron Steamer: The Bristol Steam Navigation Company, in order to afford increased and more rapid communication between Carmarthen and Bristol, have now on the stocks a new and splendid iron steamer, thirty feet longer than the 'Phoenix', which will trade between this port and Bristol on and after the 1st of April, 1853. She will probably be the swiftest boat in the channel and will be fitted up with all the recent improvements. She will be constructed so as to come up to the Quay every time she comes into port.

The urge to push the railway to the far west was stimulated by the development of Milford Haven as an intercontinental port. The Eastern Steam Navigation Company and the Australian Direct (via Panama)[11] Steam Navigation Company, for example, catered for the rapidly expanding emigration to Australia, which owed not a little to the gold-rush then in full swing there. It took only fifteen months for the railhead to arrive in Haverfordwest, and it would have arrived earlier but for the difficulties over the bridging of the Towy at Carmarthen.

The Admiralty had a big say in the kind of bridge that could be placed over a shipping lane, and a swing bridge was settled upon, but even this would need piers in the waterway. The fears expressed by the ships' masters of the town seemed to be confirmed by the report that:

> . . . as the 'Star' steamer was coming up to the quay, she struck against one of the pillars of the railway bridge and was considerably damaged. Captain Jackson took every precaution to avoid an accident, and when the steamer struck the pillar she was not being propelled by the paddles, but only carried against it by the force of the stream. The damage to the pillar was soon repaired and the bridge is now making rapid progress. Two of the pillars are finished and the central one is nearly completed. A number of men are busily employed on rivetting the ironwork.

The bridge was completed by December, 1853, and trains and ships more or less happily co-existed right through to the time eighty years later when the iron bridge swung down for

Sailing ships carried the bulk of Carmarthen's cargo: Alongside the Bulwarks, opposite Carmarthen Quay. *(Carmarthen Museum).*

Setting the sails and catching the tide. *(Carmarthen Museum).*

the last time, over the wake of Carmarthen's last departing coaster.

On a warm July evening in 1865, a great crowd gathered around the Pothouse Quay, drawn by the news of an event by then sadly rare in the Port of Carmarthen . . . a launching. It was the first for fifteen years, and though they could not know it, the last ever, but the traditional Carmarthen welcome for a home-built ship was undiminished, for the people still loved their river and saw it as their principal trading highway, despite the inroads which the railway was making into its traffic. The *Carmarthen Journal* recorded the launch of the pleasure steamer 'Lily':

> Monday evening [the 24th of July, 1865] will long be remembered by the people of Carmarthen as being the occasion for the launch of the steamboat 'Lily' the property of Mr. E. N. H. Davies of this town. Too much credit cannot be given to such a praiseworthy and plucky undertaking, taking into consideration that no vessel of any sort has been launched here for the past fifteen years [the last being the 'William' built by Messrs. Phillips and Lewis].[12]
>
> Mr. Davies, who has been a sailor nearly all his life, having conceived the idea that a small and cheaply constructed steamboat to ply between Carmarthen and the Ferryside (and Tenby if necessary) would be a boon to the inhabitants of the town, and unaided by any individual, he commissioned Mr. John George, carpenter, a native of the town, to build him a craft. Mr. George designed the lines and at once commenced work.
>
> The dimensions of the 'Lily' are as follows: Length of keel 68 feet, length overall 75 feet, beam 12 feet. She is 'Clipper' built and has a quarter-deck and saloon aft. She is schooner rigged and is of 12 horse-power, her engines propelling a screw. Draught of water 3 feet to 3½ feet, and about 18 inches forward. Her figurehead is a cherubic child holding in its right hand a Lily held against its brow.
>
> Throughout the day cannon boomed from the Pothouse, and the vessels and other boats on the river were gaily decorated with bunting. By about six o'clock both sides of the river were lined with a large concourse of spectators eager to witness the launch, which was most successful.
>
> An amateur band under the leadership of Mr. W. Evans played several pieces of favourite music from Mr. Davies's yacht 'Eagle', which was moored in the middle of the river, and the 'Lily', with

Mr. Davies and several friends on board, was towed across the river and then up to the Quay near the Custom House, where she was moored.

The assembly then dispersed, after giving several hearty cheers for Mr. Davies. At about half past eight o'clock about 120 gentlemen, including about 50 of Mr. Davies's workmen, sat down to a capital supper prepared by Mrs. Thomas, hostess of the Lamb Inn in her best style.

It was inevitable that the march of progress would eventually overtake the coastal shipping trade, and it was equally inevitable that a town that could earn such scathing criticism from a Parliamentary Commission over its neglect of its river would eventually turn its back on it altogether. In fact, the inroads which the railways began to make into the west Wales coasting trade after 1852 soon shaded into the picture of apathy that had long plagued the River Towy, and it was somewhat in that spirit that, in November, 1867, the *Welshman* newspaper declared:

> We will not indulge in dreams of a busy port with large returns in Carmarthen. We know that at one time a decent trade was done here and that the future is not so dreary as it is occasionally represented. The river is better than many that are always filled with shipping, and it is capable of considerable improvement. The town itself is a natural centre of a populous agricultural country and is already the terminus of several railways traversing the entire district.[13] That being the case, is it not probable that this port will do a larger trade than it has done for many years past?

Despite the *Welshman*'s pessimistic, almost pleading tone, there could still be as many as twenty shipping movements—nearly all of them sailing ships—in and out of the port in the course of a week, to and from London, Bristol, Shoreham, Bideford, Barnstaple, Aberystwyth, Milford, Llanelli and Swansea. And Carmarthen was a calling place on a regular Irish service by the Bristol Steam Navigation Company's 'Firefly' between Bristol, Tenby, Milford and Wexford. Even so, the port dues being collected in Carmarthen amounted to no more than £35 a year, a fact accounted for by a practice dating right back to the days before municipal government reform in 1835 curtailed the privileges enjoyed by the town's burgesses. One of the perks overlooked in the clean-up was that of exemption from port dues, a facility eagerly exploited by the old burgesses' successors, and:

> . . . when the newly created burgesses claimed exemption, and although they had no legal right to do so, the council did not interpose. The consequence is that the dues have not been paid except in a few instances by the burgesses of the town, and the revenue which ought to be £400 a year is reduced to the paltry sum of £35.

One of the consequences of this was the continued neglect of the river and the quay, which caused the *Welshman* in its concern for the future of the port to exclaim "Is there no improvement to be made in the river, no fords to be removed, no extension of the Quay?" . . . while the borough council was busily engaged with plans to scrap port dues altogether!

## NOTES

[1] An authority on naval history told the author that this incident was probably unique in the experience of the Press-gang.

[2] There is a supreme and apparently unconscious irony in the choice of name for the three-lane highway that now separates the town from its river. The road was carved through the area of the quay that once housed Carmarthen's oldest families—the coracle people—and the authorities were persuaded to call it . . . Coracle Way!

[3] Still open for business on the quay.

[4] *Militia Order Books,* Dyfed Archive Services, Carmarthen.

[5] See page 112.

[6] Two weeks pay for a policeman.

[7] Stage coach connections.

[8] *English Social History,* G. M. Trevelyan, O.M., (Longmans, Green & Co. Ltd., London, 1944).

[9] Trevelyan, op. cit.

[10] The Corporation was severely criticised for its neglect of the river over many years, in the report of the Parliamentary Commission on Municipal Corporations in England and Wales, published in 1834 (copy in the National Library of Wales).

[11] Overland across the Isthmus of Panama; the Panama Canal was still sixty years away.

[12] The steam tug 'William' was launched in April, 1847, by Mrs. Jackson, wife of the Master of the 'Phoenix' paddle steamer which ran between Carmarthen and Bristol. A powerful little tug for her time, on one occasion she towed three sailing ships down the Towy and out to the bar, being "loudly cheered by a great many persons who had assembled to witness her departure".

[13] Carmarthen was by now connected by rail with Aberystwyth, Milford Haven, Pembroke Dock, Tenby, Cardigan, Llandeilo and Mid-Wales, North-Pembrokeshire, and through south-east Wales to London.

The impact of the railways on coastal shipping had at first been more psychological than real and it soon began to dawn on some port authorities that something might be done about it. As the *Welshman* explained:

> In the North of England the rapid progress of railways led some towns to neglect the rivers which at one time were the principal means of communication with distant places, especially for the carriage of heavy goods. It was thought that the railway would supersede every other means of conveyance. In fact, no one supposed it possible that coasting vessels could compete with the railway, but the shrewd men of Lancashire and Yorkshire were not long in discovering that they had overestimated the carrying powers of railways and doggedly set about restoring the ports.

It was a message that did not get through to the Carmarthen authorities until it was too late. The Bristol Steam Navigation Company, whose paddle steamers, the mainstay of the port and of the western coasting trade, had plied between Bristol, Carmarthen and Pembrokeshire for over forty years suddenly announced the immediate cessation of its Carmarthen service. The 'Undine', the last of a line of elegant paddle steamers that had for so long been a part of life on the river and in the town, would come no more. Reflecting the shock felt in the town, the *Carmarthen Journal* reported on the 29th of April, 1870:

> The intelligence has taken the inhabitants of Carmarthen by surprise. Even the small town of Cardigan maintains a steamer newly built for coastal traffic, while Aberystwyth and Aberaeron enjoy direct water communication with Bristol itself. The strange contrast is increased by local circumstances. The population of Carmarthen is 10,000 and the port is free, Quay Dues having been abolished two years ago. Moreover there is an extensive back-country extending as far as Tregaron to be supplied with goods, with railway accommodation complete. Nor is the district of north-west Cardiganshire that alone which patronises the steamer 'Undine'. She also visited Tenby and carried goods for the interjacent country.
>
> Is the goods traffic to and from Bristol to be handed over to the railway? Monopolisation is hardly adapted to the commercial interests of the nineteenth century.[1] There is greater security in competition. We hail with pleasure the prosperity of the Great

> Western Railway Company, but this topic has its public as well as its private and proprietary aspects. Viewed in this light the withdrawal of the 'Undine' steamer will be a great injury.
>
> The Bristol Steam Navigation Company propose as a substitute to convey goods by their Irish steamers, which will call at Tenby and Milford. The cargo for Carmarthen and the country above will be landed and conveyed to the station at Tenby, or sent by lighter to the pontoon at Neyland, afterwards hoisted to the platform and stowed in trucks for Carmarthen &c. It is difficult to see how Carmarthen consignees can possibly take a favourable view of their proposals.
>
> This town cannot do without a steamer.

Thus was Carmarthen taken out of the mainstream of the still quite extensive coasting trade in a rebuff from which she never really recovered. But there were still some individual entrepreneurs who would in their turn keep open the river lifeline for many years yet—entrepreneurs like Mr. Pockett of Swansea, who two months afterwards stepped into the breach with his paddle vessels 'Prince of Wales' and 'Velindre' and his screw steamer 'The Henry Southan' to run a fortnightly service, with the promise of one or more a week "if the public will so far patronise him as to require further facilities". As an introduction to his service, Mr. Pockett, through his Carmarthen agents Bagnall and Son, went so far as to announce that on the 30th of June, 1870, his 'Prince of Wales' would sail from Carmarthen on an excursion trip to Tenby and the Stack Rocks "returning in good time by the evening tide".

Even so, an air of gloom continued to pervade discussion about the state of trade in the port, with the *Carmarthen Journal* nostalgically remembering that:

> There was a time 'within the memory of the oldest inhabitants' when this town was the chief seaport of the county and when a large and substantial coasting trade was carried on with Bristol and other large seaport towns.
>
> The opening of the Llanelli railway tended to divert much of the traffic from the River Towy, but the culmination of the causes which nearly annihilated the shipping trade of this port was the opening of the South Wales Railway to Carmarthen.
>
> Such is the decadence of the shipping interest that about six is the maximum number of vessels belonging to the town [as compared with about sixty half a century before]. It is also very

difficult to charter a vessel to come to Carmarthen for several reasons. The principal one is the uncertainty of a return freight. There is also wanting that valuable adjunct so very necessary to the quick despatch of vessels inward and outward, namely a steam tug.

In short, such is the combination of adverse circumstances that Carmarthen as a seaport has nigh become 'A thing of the past'.

The same could be said of shipbuilding on the river and the celebrations traditionally accompanying a launch, of which dim memories were sometimes revived by a rare, if comparatively small, event such as the launch of a yacht built for the Mayor in 1869. As the *Carmarthen Journal* observed:

> Shipbuilding at Carmarthen has gone out of fashion, but an instance occurs occasionally as a sort of reminder of bygone days. At 8 o'clock on Monday evening [12th July] a yacht built for His Worship the Mayor by Mr. John George and carrying about 15 tons, was launched at the Quay in the presence of a goodly number of spectators. The booming of cannon was heard for a full hour previous to the event and three discharges in instant succession greeted the first motion of the yacht towards the water. Amid loud cheers she plunged herself into the stream bearing herself proudly afloat. The Mayor received the hearty congratulations of many present at the successful launch. We hear it is intended as soon as possible to give the yacht a trip to Ilfracombe.

Mr. Pockett's 'Velindre' (seen here in the Bristol Channel) came onto the Carmarthen service in 1870. *(Grahame Farr. West Country Passenger Steamers).*

The paddle steamer 'Privateer', a frequent visitor to Carmarthen in the late 19th century. Seen here at Bideford in 1885.

*(Grahame Farr. West Country Passenger Steamers).*

But isolated events raised hopes for a better future:

> It is said that just before dawn the darkness of the night is intensest. We rejoice that a glimmering hope appears on the horizon of the 'Old Port' in the shape of a powerful steam barge, which is intended to assist the shipping in the river by towing them up and down and aiding them to discharge their cargoes during the neap tides at Black Pool or Ferryside. It will likewise give a valuable boon to our enterprising neighbour Mr. Pockett, as well as to the tradesmen of the town generally, because it will realise the long desired hope of securing a 'weekly trip' instead of fortnightly as at present [by the steamship 'Henry Southan']. Anything calculated to revive the languished trade of the port is a matter for congratulation and we hail the advent of the steam barge with much satisfaction.

The owners of the Carmarthen Tinworks—Thomas, Lester and Company—were anxious that Carmarthen should not be without a regular service of vessels of a size capable of carrying their tinplate, so they commissioned the steam barge, to be built at W. H. Nevill's Wern Ironworks in Llanelli. She was 52 feet long, of 16 feet beam, with an engine and two boilers producing twelve horse power, and with her heavy steam crane she performed yeoman service on the river for many years after her arrival in 1870.

Thomas, Lester and Company even had a sea-going vessel of their own. She was the clipper-built schooner 'Merlin', one of the six ships registered in the Port of Carmarthen, but the company was less lucky with that enterprise. The 'Merlin' was lost with an uninsured cargo of tinplate worth £4,000 when she was cut in two by an Irish ferry steamer in Holyhead Bay on the 15th of October, 1874. Her Master, Captain Jenkins, and his crew—two of them also Carmarthen men—were saved.

On that note one might pause to consider just how hard was the life of a seafarer and how merciless the sea in the day of the sailing ship and the small coastal paddler. It has been calculated that in the seventeen years from 1849 to 1866, twenty thousand British merchant ships were lost, with countless lives. On one terrible night alone, the night of the 25th of October, 1859, two hundred and twenty three vessels were wrecked around the coasts of Britain, with the loss of eight hundred lives. Four contemporary reports catalogue just one of the many losses on that graveyard of shipping on Carmarthen's own front door step—Cefn Sidan Sands—and show that the Dynion y Bwyelli Bach were still very much in business in 1886:

(1)

Great storms and floods. Terrible loss of life. Immense damage to property. Few storms in recent years have equalled the severity of that experienced throughout the southern and western parts of Wales during Friday and Saturday last. From all points have come reports detailing the great havoc which was caused by the hurricane which prevailed, and those in great part refer to casualties along the Welsh coast.

Sad wreck in Carmarthen bay. Eighteen lives lost. A disaster resulting in loss of life which fortunately in late years has been seldom paralleled in Carmarthen Bay occurred on Cefn Sidan Sands on Friday. The steel built, four-masted, full-rigged vessel 'Teviotdale' of Glasgow, 1,673 tons register, James Smith, Master, left Cardiff on Thursday evening with a crew of twenty-nine hands and a full cargo of coal for Bombay. The tugboat which took the ship out of port parted company with her about 10.30 on Thursday night when the gale was well on. During the night the ship lost most of her canvas and about 6.30 on Friday morning she took a roll and shifted her cargo. The vessel continued shipping water till about 10 o'clock [Friday morning] when an attempt was made to square away and run back to Penarth Roads. It is probable that the master lost his reckoning, for instead of making Penarth Roads the crew found themselves in a short time on the dreaded Cefn Sidan Sands in Carmarthen Bay [over seventy miles to the west!].

The Captain called all hands together to heave the lead and it is reported that he admonished them to be handy, for they would be ashore in a few moments. The lead showed that there were ten fathoms of water, and half an hour later the ship took ground opposite Saint Ishmael's. Three of the boats were rendered useless, but the ship's lifeboat was successfully lowered about midday and the Captain and the Second and Third Officers, thirteen men and three boys crowded into her. In a short time the boat got broadside on and this was the last seen of her by those on board the vessel.

Two of the boat's company got on shore alive somewhere between Kidwelly and Pembrey, the rest being drowned. After the boat left the ship the only hope for those left on board was that the people on shore would be attracted by the rockets fired and the lights burned and that help would come out. About three o'clock in the afternoon the men set the foresail to try to get the ship further over the bank, but it was torn away and completed the loss of all the ship's canvas. The vessel laid helpless at the mercy of the terrific sea and an attempt was made by one of the crew, an Italian, to float a small raft, which resulted in its being immediately swamped while its maker narrowly escaped with his life.

About midnight Friday [nearly twelve hours after the 'Teviotdale' struck the sands] the Ferryside lifeboat was got out under the command of Coxswain Mr. William Thomas, and reached the vessel about three o'clock in the morning. A great deal of difficulty was experienced in getting the men off, but the task was successfully accomplished and the men and their rescuers reached the shore in safety.

* * *

(2)

Sergeant Lewis Hughes reports that he summoned the Jury and attended the Inquest at the Town Hall on the body of James Smith, Master of the ship 'Teviotdale' of Glasgow, which was driven onto Cefn Sidan Sands on the night of Friday 15th October. Verdict of the Jury—Found in the River Towy in the Parish of Llandefeilog, Carmarthenshire.[2]

* * *

(3)

The Chief Constable, Sergeants Williams and Hughes, P.Cs Stacey 1, Phillips 2, Burnhill 6, Arthur 7 and Jones 8, also Mr. George Rogers and his workmen and Mr. Joseph the Undertaker, met at the mortuary at 5.30 a.m., took the body of James Smith, late master of the ship 'Teviotdale', put it in a hearse and accompanied the body to the Town Railway Station, and was put on a truck of the L. & N.W. Railway Co., which left at 6.20 a.m. to be taken to Banffshire, Scotland.[3]

* * *

(4)

The wreck of the 'Teviotdale'. At Llanelli Petty Sessions on Wednesday, before Messrs. R. McLaren and H. Child Buckley—Henry Evans, Kidwelly, William Jenkins, Kidwelly, Thomas Morgan, Kidwelly, John Jones, Llansaint and John Evans, Llansaint, were summoned for having in their possession certain articles belonging to the crew of the 'Teviotdale', which was wrecked on Cefn Sidan Sands on the 15th of October last.

Mr. Frederick Cooke, Llanelli Customs, was for the prosecution. The Bench inflicted heavy fines in each case and said it was a most cruel thing to rob shipwrecked sailors of their property.[4]

* * *

Strandings were a frequent problem on the River Towy, too, and the loss involved could be considerable, as it was when the 150 ton French brigantine 'Eugenie Maria' settled on the bank near Black Pool in October, 1879, and was virtually wrecked. Two Carmarthen pilots, John Rees and John Jones, managed to free and refloat her and to bring her to the quay . . . where vessel and cargo of potatoes were auctioned for £20! The Llanelli Steam Navigation Company's "fast new iron screw steamer" 'Cambria', commanded by William Thomas, was more fortunate when she stranded in January, 1875, despite the fact that she had to remain on the bank for several days before she could be refloated on a spring tide.

Although a good deal of dredging was done, particularly in the winter months when it provided work for many of the coraclemen outside the fishing season and a source of sand and gravel for the town, it was nowhere near enough to cope with the problem. So bad had it become by 1892 that the paddle steamer 'Tivyside' grounded three times in the half mile between the swing bridge and the quay, even though the tide was full, drawing the comment that "what little shipping there is on the Towy will disappear altogether if the authorities do not remove these banks which have accumulated in the bed of the river". But it fell on deaf ears.

Even so, as the nineteenth century drew to its close, in a good week Carmarthen Quay could still boast half a dozen sailing ships alongside at a time, as well as the occasional foreign steamer. It was largely dependent on the height of the tides, as is seen from an item in the *Welshman* of the 7th of September, 1894:

> Shipping at Carmarthen Quay: The high tides that prevail about this season have brought a large number[5] of craft to Carmarthen Quay. The following were to be seen there on Saturday evening (1st September): The 'Da Capo' (Sandesvaal) and brigantine 'Harold' (Friedrichstadt) with timber for Mr. Joseph, the latter being tugged in by the 'Hero' of Llanelli; the 'King Ja Ja' from Bristol with 2,000 sacks of flour and barley for Mr. Arthur; the schooner 'Dorothea' (Caernarvon) with slates, and 'Esther' (Beaumaris) from New Ross, Ireland, with 100 tons of paving flags, and the schooner 'Hilda' (Chester) from Connah's Quay with 200 tons of floor and ridge tiles for Mr. Charles Jones, The Quay, and the S.S. 'Tivyside', which made three or four trips during the week with cargoes for Mr. Jenkins.
>
> Among the other vessels here near the same time were the S.S. 'Alpha' (a German vessel) from Portishead with 1,000 sacks of maize for Mr. Arthur, and the smack 'Nautilus' loaded with a full cargo from Mr. Arthur to Laugharne.

There were summer steamer excursions to Tenby and Milford and around the Stack Rocks, and the regular weekly steamship connections with the Bristol Channel ports by the 'Cambria', the 'Neath Abbey' or the 'Tivyside', while the

**A good week on Carmarthen Quay at the end of the 19th century.**
*(Emlyn Jones).*

steamships 'Ibis' or the 'Lady Kate' sailed fortnightly between Carmarthen and Liverpool, the gateway to the New World, held invitingly open by a fiercely competitive emigrant trade offering such attractions as:

> The only direct line of steamers to Philadelphia: The American Line United States Mail Steamers from Liverpool every Wednesday, calling at Queenstown [now Cobh, in Cork Harbour]. First-class full-powered iron steamships, the 'Lord Clive', 'Illinois', 'British Empire', 'Indiana' and 'Pennsylvania'. Cabin passage twelve guineas [£12.60p] to eighteen guineas [£18.90p]—return tickets at reduced rates. Steerage passage[6] as low as by any other fast line, including an ample supply of provisions. Steerage passengers are forwarded to New York or Boston without additional charge. Intermediate[7] passage, including beds, bedding and all necessary utensils and separate table, eight guineas [£8.40p].

It was not only from Liverpool that emigrants from Carmarthen and its hinterland could cross the Atlantic. Cardiff offered:

> Direct steam communication between the Bristol Channel and the United States of America and Canada: The South Wales Atlantic Steamship Company's new first-class full-powered Clyde-

built steamships 'The Glamorgan', 2,500 tons 500 h.p., 'The Pembroke', 2,500 tons 400 h.p., 'The Carmarthen', 3,000 tons 600 h.p., or other first class steamers will sail regularly between Cardiff and New York.

While the Great Western Steamship Company advertised:

> Important to Welshmen: Emigration to America at Reduced Fares. The splendid steamer 'Warwick' is intended to sail from Swansea direct to New York, and their steamer 'Dorset' from Newport to Quebec direct, thus giving an excellent opportunity for passengers from Wales to reach the United States or Canada. Fares: Saloon 12 guineas [£12.60p]; Steerage 4 guineas [£4.20p]. For further information and berths apply to E. Woodman, Parade House, Carmarthen.

Throughout much of the nineteenth century, many hundreds of west Wales emigrants said goodbye for ever to their families and friends on Carmarthen Quay, caught the last sight of waving hands and handkerchiefs as they rounded the river bend beyond the railway bridge, and gathered to the memories they would take to their new lives in Canada, America, Australia or New Zealand, the lush green fields and woods lining the wide and wandering Towy, the commanding ruins of Llanstephan Castle at the river mouth and—from the

**Llanstephan Castle, the last sight on the River Towy for emigrants sailing from Carmarthen Quay.** *(Emlyn Jones).*

The S.S. 'Merthyr' approaching the quay through the railway swing bridge. *(National Library of Wales).*

stern rail behind the thrashing paddle wheels—the last faint sound of the bells of Saint Ishmael's drifting across the water, following them to the sand bar and the expanse of the Bristol Channel.

One little ship whose regular visits to Carmarthen Quay linked the nineteenth century with the twentieth was the S.S. 'Merthyr'. She ran for many years between Bristol and Carmarthen, her main cargoes being of flour for local mills, carried onto the quay in sacks down the narrow gang plank by the bag carriers. The old 'Merthyr' is still remembered in and around the town with great affection as a "very, very clean boat" with polished engines and freshly painted rails, and her Captain Everett is remembered as a well-respected and perfect gentleman. Many in the town had the pleasure, if tide, train times and weather permitted, of a trip down the river of an evening, to be taken off at Ferryside by the pilot boat for the train journey back to town, and many others were taken by the friendly Captain all the way to Bristol if they had business there. And the bag carriers? One whose memory went back to the first years of this century remembered them: "Their back teeth awash and drunk as lords, the more beer they imbibed, the steadier they ran; surely", he says "God looks after drunken sailors!" He remembered, too, a bag carrier by the

The 'Merthyr' and two sailing ships at low water. *(Sid Jones)*.

The 'Merthyr' tows a sailing ship down river. *(Carmarthen Museum)*.

The bag carriers and others on the quay. One-armed Jack "Stumpy" is seen in the doorway on the right, with a sack on his shoulders.
*(Terry James, Rampart Press, Carmarthen).*

name of Stumpy, "One arm holding the bag and the stump waving to keep his balance." Stumpy, it was said, had had his arm chopped off by a Zulu at Rorke's Drift![8]

It was the outbreak of the first world war that put the seal on the end of Carmarthen as a port, as the coasting trade was largely suspended because of other demands on shipping and because of enemy submarine activity around the western coasts and the western approaches. Its resumption after the war found Carmarthen reduced to a mere two ships a year. Although in 1928 the number had risen to thirty-five in the year—all small vessels of an average of some 70 tons each—only four foreign ships tied up at the quay over the last eighteen years of Carmarthen's existence as a port. From 1928 the decline sharpened to the point where, in 1938, the sight of a ship on the river was rare indeed, only one little steamer paying only five visits to Carmarthen quay.

One day in that year, a small group of people stood on the quay outside the Jolly Tar pub, idly watching as a dirty old 250 ton coal burner puffed her way out into the river on the rising tide and headed down towards the sea. Neither she nor any other ships would see that river again.

Carmarthen was a port no more.

NOTES

[1] The construction of the Manchester Ship Canal (1887-1894) was the result of the appreciation of this by the merchants and shippers of the north west of England.

[2] *Occurrence Book,* Carmarthen Borough Police, Wednesday 27th October, 1886. Dyfed Archive Services, Carmarthen Museum Collection.

[3] *Occurrence Book,* Carmarthen Borough Police, Friday 29th October, 1886. Dyfed Archive Services, Carmarthen Museum Collection.

[4] *Carmarthen Journal,* 19th November, 1886.

[5] To describe 6 sailing ships and 3 steamers in a week as a "large number" is in itself indicative of the normal state of trade in the Port of Carmarthen.

[6] Communal, cramped and very basic accommodation in which individuals and families provided for their own food, cooking and washing for a matter of £3 or £4.

[7] A cut above 'Steerage', but much inferior to cabin accommodation.

[8] Sir John Williams of Melbourne, Australia, who left Carmarthen in 1910 to go to sea. Others attribute the loss of Stumpy's arm to a circular saw in the sawmills.

The paddle steamer 'Tivyside' heads down river as time runs out for the Port of Carmarthen . . . and for herself. She was wrecked on the Gower coast on 14th June, 1900. *(Carmarthen Museum).*

# Contrasts

''This is a new reign'' said Egremont. ''Perhaps it is a new era.'' ''I think so'' said the younger stranger. ''Well, society may be in its infancy'' said Egremont, slightly smiling, ''But say what you like, our Queen reigns over the greatest nation that ever existed.'' ''Which nation?'' asked the younger stranger, ''For she reigns over two.'' The stranger paused. Egremont was silent, but looked inquiringly. ''Yes,'' resumed the younger stranger after a moment's interval, ''Two nations; between whom there is no intercourse and no sympathy; who are as ignorant of each other's habits, thoughts and feelings as if they were dwellers in different zones, or inhabitants of different planets; who are formed by different breeding, are fed by a different food, are ordered by different manners, and are not governed by the same laws.'' ''You speak of . . .?'' said Egremont, hesitatingly.

''The Rich and the Poor''.

Benjamin Disraeli (Sybil, 1845)

# TWO NATIONS

In the first years of the nineteenth century, when Britain fought Napoleon, there were two sides to the Carmarthen coin. A prosperous side showed in the principal streets of the town —Lammas Street, Guildhall Square, Market Street, King Street and Spilman Street—which presented a picture of bustle, vitality and prosperity befitting a busy seaport, a centre of road communications, a booming agricultural market town and a place whose industries thrived on the demands of a nation at war. Carmarthen was the meeting place of the gentry and the country squires, for whom the coaching inns provided the best in food, drink and entertainments. And behind all the bustle of the streets and the boisterousness of the townspeople lay the buttresses of that prosperity: the merchants, shipbuilders and shopkeepers, the tinplate and ironmasters, the hatters, tanners, cabinet makers, maltsters, seedsmen, printers and bookbinders. A trade directory of the time lists over forty such, and since commerce, property and trade will always provide fruitful fields for them, the town could boast of no fewer than sixteen attorneys at law.

As early as 1804 Carmarthen was served by a regular weekly newspaper, the *Cambrian,* published at Swansea and the first weekly newspaper to be published in Wales, to be followed in 1810 by its own, the *Carmarthen Journal*, which flourishes to this day. Those early newspapers concerned themselves far less with local 'tittle-tattle' than with national and international, legal and financial, shipping and commercial news, which they conveyed to eager readers at a speed which is surprising given the remoteness of west Wales from the mainstream of the political, commercial, social and cultural life of the time.

All of this, while in the dark, damp and fetid hovels of the riverside, of the steep and narrow terraces between the quay and the town and of the warren that was its back streets, the greater part of the population was living four and five families to a tiny cottage and seven or eight people to a bed. Here disease was rife and death came early. Here, too, fully a third

Carmarthen, early in the nineteenth century. *(Carmarthen Museum)*.

One of the steep and narrow passages connecting the town with the riverside.
*(Carmarthen Museum).*

of the town's five thousand or so inhabitants had no other source of subsistence but what salmon and sewin they could net from the river, from their four hundred coracles.

There were indeed two nations—the privileged and the people, the former holding all the power and all the comforts and benefits that power bestows and the latter having nothing but whatever bare subsistence they might scrape in a hostile world over which they had not the least control. The story of 19th century Carmarthen is the story of how those two nations were brought closer together, for whatever social injustices remained at the end of the century, they were as nothing to those under which the 'lower orders' lived when that century opened.

It was in the 'natural order' of things in the rigid class system of those times that the gulf between the 'two nations' could be bridged only by charity of the most paternalistic kind, even in times of 'prosperity'. Developing this paradox, an economist wrote that:

> To talk of the prosperous state of the country under such a condition of things [the Napoleonic war] involves a palpable contradiction. It would be more correct to liken the situation of the

> community to that of the inhabitants of a town subjected to a general conflagration, in which some became suddenly enriched by carrying off the valuables, while the masses were involved in ruin and destitution.[1]

For all its beneficial effects on agriculture, trade and industry, the war meant high prices and a steep fall in the value of wages. The war and its aftermath were economically disastrous for the poor. As another writer observed:

> . . . of all the classes that bore the burdens of the war and paid the penalty of their rulers' errors, no class was so destitute of compensations as the class that could only make its voice heard by food riots and by the kind of demonstration that ended in a cavalry charge and half a dozen men sent to the gallows.[2]

The relationship between wages and the cost of food can be judged by the fact that a Carmarthen labourer in 1800 would be lucky to earn six shillings [30p] a week, which would buy for him and his large family ten pounds of bread, or two gallons of wheat, or just over two and a half 'dishes' of potatoes—and no more. Fresh meat, or indeed anything but the most basic of food, was unknown among the poor.[3] If he did not earn, he and his family would subsist on scavenging or charity, or they would starve. Malnutrition was a very large element in the short life-expectancy of the poor.

Such was the shortage of grain for staple foods in December, 1800, that King George III issued a proclamation prohibiting the giving of oats to any but work-horses, and forbidding the use of pastry. The proclamation was 'cried' through the town by the Common Crier, and read from the pulpit in Saint Peter's Church. Food shortages, high prices, low wages and sudden unemployment were the causes of frequent riots and attacks on corn stores and food warehouses. Carmarthen was a scene of distress and turmoil at the turn of the century, and full of soldiers, whose bayonets and bullets were the only effective weapon available to the authorities. In the Spring of 1801, for example, there were no less than seventeen military formations in the little town—not only battalions of the Carmarthenshire Volunteers, but also units of the West Glamorgan Volunteers and the 'Swansea and Gower Legion', together with several detachments of regular army regiments.

The townspeople had enough problems of their own, but

they frequently had to cope with mobs of distressed country people, colliers and ironworkers from the surrounding area, coming to Carmarthen to register their desperation by rioting. In April, 1801, for example, there was great fear in the town when the town bell rang on top of the Market Cross,[4] drums beat the call to arms, and troops rushed to the town approaches to head off a marching mob of rioting colliers. Such food riots were to be a feature of life in Carmarthen for a good many years to come, one notable eruption being the Cheese Riot of October, 1818. Summoned again by the ringing of the town bell, and incensed by rumours that while they starved the town's merchants were about to ship cargoes of cheese from the quay, the people of the riverside and the mean streets of Carmarthen swarmed onto the quay, boarded the sailing ships and began to throw their cargoes back onto the quayside. This "numerous and tumultuous assemblage of the lower class of inhabitants of the town" attacked the magistrates while the Mayor tried to read the proclamation from the Riot Act,[5] and only the timely arrival of cavalry in the shape of the 1st Carmarthen Troop of the Yeomanry Cavalry, under Captain Jones, the 'Derllys' troop of Yeomanry Cavalry under Captain Howel, and the Carmarthen Militia under Captain Harding, saved the day. Curiously enough—and completely at odds with the fury of the mob—very little of the cheese was stolen, most of it being returned to the warehouses, on the promise of the merchants to sell it in Carmarthen after all!

The masses were excluded from all opportunity for discussion and political association, because Britain was no democracy[6] and the establishment sensed revolution in the air. Indeed the men of property equated the very word democracy with anarchy and revolution, and they took all the steps necessary to suppress any such dangerous thoughts and to resist any demand for popular participation in government. As late as 1831, during the often violent agitation for electoral reform, Britain had a Prime Minister who knew just how to deal with that kind of thing. The Duke of Wellington was probably the best proof of the adage that great soldiers rarely, if ever, make great politicians. To him a battle was a battle, and the tactics little different whether the enemy was the French or a rioting mob of urban workers. Summing up all the fears of the establishment, the Iron Duke expressed the opinion that

> A democracy has never been established in any part of the world that has not immediately declared war against property and against all the principles of conservation which are secured by, and are in fact the principal objects of, the British Constitution as it now exists. Property and its possessors will become the common enemy.[7]

In fairness to the old soldier, whose political career died with the victory of the Reformers, his was not the only government, and Britain's was not the only ruling establishment that was haunted by the spectre of the French Revolution.

The masses were excluded from education, which was seen by many of the upper classes as tending to discontent and the overthrow of orderly society. As a nineteenth century Lord Chief Justice (Lord Cockburn) put it: 'The principle is reverenced and indisputable that the ignorance of the people is necessary to their obedience to the law'.

Exclusion from politics and education was backed up by savage laws designed to protect the interests of property. Over two hundred offences ranging from minor theft and poaching to murder attracted the death penalty, and for much of the century sentences of transportation 'beyond the seas' for seven or fourteen years, and even for life, for what are now petty crimes, were a regular feature of Carmarthen's Assize calendars. Another nineteenth century Judge embellished his pronouncement of yet another death sentence with an exposition of the theory behind the severity of the law: "There is no hope," he said "of regenerating a felon in this life. His continued existence would merely diffuse a corrupting influence. It is better for his own sake, as well as for society, that he should be hanged." Or, as Lord Palmerston put it in 1815 when arguing against a move to abolish flogging in the armed forces: "The English,[8] owing to the freedom of their constitution and their higher feeling of personal independence, require more punishment than other nations."

So much for the reasons why there was no other country in the world "where so many and so large a variety of actions were punishable with loss of life".[9]

They were hard times indeed for the poor, but it is worth pausing to consider how they felt about their circumstances. It must be remembered that the harshness of their daily lives was something into which they were born, a state from which few sought (or even dreamed of) escape. It was "ordained" and it was largely accepted, and, particularly in the days before universal education opened a window on a wider world, the poor could be happy in their ignorance. Too often are they portrayed as unhappy wretches living lives of unrelieved gloom and despair; too often those portrayals suffer from a surfeit of twentieth century hindsight. Had those people been blessed with our social and economic aspirations they would indeed have been an unsmiling lot. But they weren't. Which explains their ability to throw their troubles to the winds when an occasion like the celebrations for a famous victory, the departure or return of a local hero, or a royal event brought a splash of colour and a burst of music into their drab existences, and to take to the streets with all the verve characteristic of nineteenth century Carmarthen.

By the 1830s, Carmarthen's population was twice that of 1801; it stood at around ten thousand, a figure that would remain more or less steady for at least a century more. This increase had been contained within roughly the same town limits, but at the cost of dense over-crowding in those parts of the town housing the 'lower orders'. For the better off, though it was towards the monument to Sir Thomas Picton, still standing in majestic isolation on the Johnstown road, that Carmarthen was extending a finger of elegant houses, while on the other side of town, superior and widely-spaced houses in their ample grounds graced the south-eastern side of Priory Street and looked out over the river from the Parade, commanding ". . . a fine and extensive view of the surrounding picturesque scenery and of the Towy, where the coracles may be seen plying about".

To the north-east of Priory Street (by now lined with houses as far as the tinworks), Waun Dew (Richmond Terrace) and its few cottages traversed open country, and the residents of Furnace House by Saint Peter's Church had an uninterrupted rural view from their ornamental gardens.

The Water Street Turnpike Gate, by the Morgan's Arms, marked the northern limit of the town buildings, and the estates of Samuel Morris at Lime Grove and Arthur Jones at

Carmarthen Assizes, held in the Guildhall: The Judge's escort of pikemen and trumpeters. *(Carmarthen Museum).*

Carmarthen Gaol, the next stop after the Assizes for those sentenced to death, transportation or imprisonment. *Des Spawton.*

Fountain Hall stood between it and Trevaughan village on the Cardigan road. Below the gate a flourishing nursery occupied the whole length of the western side of Lower Water Street, and there was still open country up beyond Saint Catherine's Mill, which still marked the extent of the development from the Water Street crossroads. The first inroad into this rural northern edge of the town was being made towards the Barnsfield by way of Tabernacle Row, not yet called Waterloo Terrace. Here was the Tabernacle, built in 1811 at the wish of the Calvanistic Baptist Minister, Titus Lewis, on the spot from which he had seen himself rise up in a dream of the Day of Judgement, and where he was to be buried before the building was begun.[10] Up beyond the Tabernacle, standing alone on the eminence of Penlan, was Carmarthen's new poor house, that gaunt, grey and forbidding edifice which was to bring misery to many in the cause of stamping out the vice of poverty and of inculcating the virtue of menial toil.

The Wide Ocean—an expanse of willow-studded marshland where now are Red Street, John Street and the Market—had been drained in 1824 and on it, on the edge of Parcyfelfet, had been built the town's important tannery, close to the new Welsh Wesleyan Chapel. Nearer the town, in a crowded area bounded by Red Street and Cambrian Place, stood the Borough Gaol, whose walls contained the watchmen's lock-up—the Roundhouse. There, too, were the town's slaughter house, a fine building modelled on the Abattoir of Paris, and (opposite the nearby Nelson Inn) a commodious new market house. But the main markets were still packed in and around the town centre, around the Guildhall, as they had been for all the centuries that Carmarthen had been a market town, and they were busier than ever. The fish and butter market, topped by the town fire bell, still stood at the Market Cross, as did the stocks, which would remain in use until at least the mid-1840s.

Since 1822 Carmarthen had been lit by gas made at the gas company's works on the marshland by the river to the west of the town. It was made from coal shipped in from Llanelli and Pembrey, and a local chemist named Evans had just perfected a method whereby it could be produced at as little as a third of the cost, to the benefit of the town and its inhabitants.

The ten principal streets of the town were now well lit, well paved and kept swept of horse-manure, a by-product of the horse era that provided a useful bonus for the town's treasury. An advertisement spoke of the sale:

> . . . by Auction at the Guildhall, on Tuesday the 16th of February [1830], at twelve o'clock by James James, Auctioneer, of all those several heaps of manure arising from the sweeping and cleansing of the streets, situate at the upper end of Lammas Street and on Waun Dew. Mr. William Williams of the 'Castle' Inn, Water Street, on application to him will show the several heaps.

Perhaps the residents of the "upper end of Lammas Street" were used to the proximity of those large manure heaps, but cleanliness in the 1830s was relative in any case, and the sanitation and drainage of the town still left much to be desired. A most unwholesome odour, emanating from the sewage outfalls on the river and from the mud at low water, pervaded the town in the heat of summer. A great deal of filth was tolerated, and the unhygienic conditions away from "the principal streets" tended to come to the fore only when they affected more than the poor, and when the town grew fearful of the dreaded cholera, which threatened Carmarthen in the thirties and ravaged it in the forties.

But for all that, Carmarthen prospered as the most important market town of west Wales and as a centre for the tanning industry and for the shoe and hat-making trades. Her chief manufacture, tinplate produced at the Furnace Mills close to the river below the eastern end of Priory Street, was reckoned the best in the Kingdom, and the iron foundry in Blue Street, a few yards below Dark Gate, did a brisk trade at a time when iron was king. The town possessed a paper mill, watered by the stream alongside the Glannant road, just along the fork from the Water Street Turnpike Gate, and a busy brickworks by the river above Dan y Banc. And Carmarthen's commercial vitality was underwritten by three sound banks, those of Messrs. Biddulph in Quay Street, Messrs. Morris in Spilman Street (nearly opposite a new Ivy Bush Inn[11]) and Messrs. Wilkins, Wilkins and Jones, half way along the north side of King Street.

The prosperous condition of Carmarthen at this time was reflected in the entertainments and sport provided for its

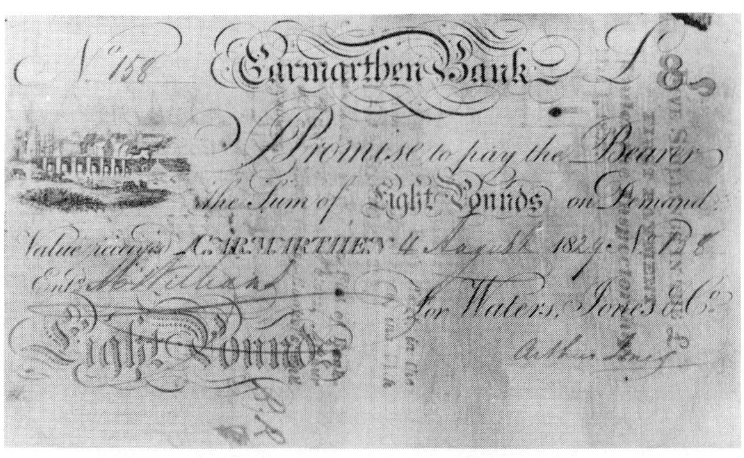

Carmarthen bank notes and tokens.

*(Carmarthen Museum. Photos by Doug Simpson).*

inhabitants, who had largely turned away from the coarser pleasures of thirty years before. While it still had its wild moments and the streets at night were rowdy, full of drunks and often violent and riotous,[12] the town could boast of such civilised attractions as horse-racing, river sports and theatrical performances, and social gatherings of the most splendid kind at the thriving coaching inns—The Boar's Head, the Red Lion, the Talbot, the Half Moon and the Nag's head, almost within touching distance of each other around the Dark Gate and below the Guildhall.[13] In September, 1830, the Carmarthen races were:

. . . superior to anything witnessed here for many years, whether we regard the running or the number and respectability of the company. The weather was delightful and the course was in excellent order, and everything seemed to conspire to increase the gratification of the numerous spectators who were present. The equippages on the course[14] passed all previous exhibitions of the kind, and the arrangements reflected great credit on the stewards, the Hon. George Rice-Trevor and Charles Morgan Esquire.

The excitement of the races was supplemented in Race Week by two "numerously and respectably attended" balls, one at the Ivy Bush and the other at the Boar's Head, and one can be sure that the rest of the town's one hundred and fifty or so alehouses and inns were equally well patronised during the week.

On the River Towy in the same month, the annual boat

"When iron was king": Workmen's tokens of the early nineteenth century, exchangeable in Carmarthen shops.
*Carmarthen Musuem (photos by Doug Simpson)*

races attracted great crowds to the quay and the river banks. Valuable cash prizes brought all classes of the inhabitants onto the river to compete in large and small rowing boats and coracles, and there was even a special event ". . . to be rowed for by cockle-girls, with no more than two oars in each boat". So numerous were the events and entries that they occupied the river between the Jolly Tar and Llyngey Pool for two days on the evening tides.

Carmarthen's long-promised new theatre in King Street replaced the stable-like building with which the theatre-going public had had to be content for many years, and some fine performances, equal to those of the big cities, were brought to it. Opening on the 7th of September, 1830, under the patronage of R. G. Thomas, Esquire, High Sheriff of the County ". . . the house was well attended and the performance went off with éclat".

Cultural and educational activities were also flourishing in the town. The Royal Free School of the British and Foreign Schools Society provided free (or, to those who could pay, cheap) rudimentary education in the 'Three Rs'. There were also private 'Seminaries' and 'Academies', such as Mr. W. Johns' 'Classical, Commercial and Mathematical Academy' in King Street. And the influence of religion grew apace; of the eleven churches and chapels built in Carmarthen in the first half of the nineteenth century, five were already well-established —Lammas Street Chapel (Heol Awst), the English Wesleyan Chapel off Red Street, the Tabernacle, Water Street Chapel (Heol Dŵr) and the Welsh Wesleyan Chapel on the drained "Wide Ocean". Their Sunday Schools were sowing the first seeds of literacy among the otherwise educationally deprived children of the 'lower orders' and while their primary purpose might have been the inculcation of the Word of God and the virtues of duty and respect for authority, they were fuelling the fires of social change. Reform, Rebeccaism, Chartism and the birth of trades unions owed much to those first elements of mass-literacy.

There was plenty of work for those capable of it . . . jobs in all the service industries that went with a busy agricultural market town, the hotels, the inns, the breweries, the stables and blacksmiths' shops, the warehouses and the shops, the tanneries, the weaving sheds, the hat and shoemaking shops, on the horse waggons, in quayside labouring jobs, on the boats, on the river dredgers and in the brick, tin and iron works. Wages were adequate, though hours were long, and discipline firm yet paternal,[15] but with careful housekeeping, wholesome food was available and cheap in well-stocked shops and in the provision market. And though the improvidence and addiction to drink of many of the 'lower orders' still kept them in the gutter so to speak, considerable improvements had taken place in their lot since the beginning of the century.

Altogether, then, Carmarthen was an exciting and virile town. But the dark side was still there, in the lives and dwellings of the 'labouring poor', as they were referred to.[16]

It is held by some social historians that the well-to-do of the 19th century alleviated their slightly uneasy consciences in charitable acts towards the poor, whose condition, while distressful, was inevitable. They, too, were products of their time and, like the 'lower orders', accepted that which they saw as being 'ordained'. In their case, too, due allowance must be made for the values and attitudes of the time, a time when honest toil and charity were among the noblest of virtues. Was not charity the only means of helping those for whom the natural order of things had ordained such a lowly state? This lowly state was graphically illustrated by the report that:

> . . . a medical gentleman had occasion to go to the Old Priory in Carmarthen and was induced to enter the dwelling of one of its inhabitants. From the wretched and emaciated appearance of three children there, they appeared to be nothing but skin and bones, and only a few rags to cover them. On enquiring of them who their parents were &c., he learned from the eldest, a little girl, that their mother had left them two days before and had gone into the country for the purpose of begging barley from the charitable, a custom among the poor at this season of the year, and that when she departed she left them only threepence [about 1p] to subsist upon until her return.
>
> On examining this abode of poverty, he discovered that there was no bed for them to lie upon, with the exception of some filthy straw placed in a corner of the floor.

It was a typical example, and things were bad enough normally in the poor quarters of the town, but the winter of

1830-31 was an unusually harsh one, bringing snow of an average depth of three feet to an area noted for its mildness and for the absence of snow. Drifts of eight and ten feet on some parts of the roads were delaying for several hours mail coaches pulled by as many as six horses.

Such conditions brought unimaginable hardship to the poor at a time when the normal mortality rate was high and the average expectation of life only forty-one years; when one in three children died before their fifth year and when destitution and malnutrition were the common lot of the 'lower orders'. The diary of a Carmarthenshire coffin maker reveals that over a period of thirty years in the mid-nineteenth century, 37% of his work was for burials of children under ten years, and only half of his work was for people over the age of twenty.

The better-off responded as they did every year at this time, the *Carmarthen Journal* commenting that:

> The distresses of the poor must be greatly increased during the winter months, and fuel and clothing are almost as necessary for their support as food. We witness with much pleasure the good which is being done among the poor of this parish by the distribution of blankets and flannel. Our Minister, the Rev. James Griffiths, with the assistance of churchwardens, has relieved upwards of one hundred and fifty persons from the charitable bequests placed at his disposal, by supplying one hundred and twenty-four blankets and eighty-six yards of flannel made up into garments.

The insolvent debtors imprisoned in the town goal and dependent on relatives or friends for subsistence ". . . begged to return their most sincere thanks to John Jones, Esquire, M.P., for a seasonable supply of three waggon loads of coal, his usual donation at this inclement season of the year", (*Carmarthen Journal*) while they also received donations of £5 from the Venerable Archdeacon Beynon, and £5 from Rees Goring Thomas Esquire, High Sheriff of the County.

Mr. Davies, landlord of the Six Bells Inn in Saint Peter's Street, distributed two cart loads of coal to the poor women he had employed on his hay-making the previous summer, and others in the town subscribed to a fund to provide bread, meat and coal to the poor.

Perhaps the most poignant comment on the distress of the

poor came in February, 1831, in a *Carmarthen Journal* editorial on an antislavery petition collected in the town. While "... wishing with the petitioners to see slavery extinguished in all the British dependencies immediately," the Editor was "... much inclined to doubt its practicability," and his revealing conclusion was that "The condition of the slaves in our West India Colonies is one of comfort compared with that of some of our own paupers." And nothing seemed to solve the problem posed by the destitute; not charity, or parish relief, and they could not be swept under the carpet. Or could they? Advertising an emigration scheme in the *Carmarthen Journal* in 1830, Mr. Edward Powell, Surveyor and Land Agent of Brecon, believed emigration to be:

> ... worth consideration of Parish Officers, as it would be more economical to afford the means to the surplus and unemployed population, thus relieving the Parish from the heavy burthen of the poor rates.

Seven or eight sailings a month from Liverpool carried ship loads of his emigrants across the Atlantic in voyages of about twenty-five days, and this fast-growing trade caused Mr. Powell to state that a "depot agent" would be appointed in every major town in Wales.

The cost of the Atlantic crossing depended on whether the emigrant could afford to pay for food as well as for deck space, and whether he made the crossing in summer or winter. Thus the fares ranged from £6 to thirty-five shillings [£1.75p], the lower rate being for a winter passage "without provisions", with the advice that the emigrant should carry provisions for a minimum of fifty days and a maximum of seventy five. Mr. Powell's twenty-five days may perhaps be charitably described as 'advertiser's licence'! For those forced to choose the lowest fare, a ticket for a winter crossing of the North Atlantic confined the emigrant to the crowded and fetid lower decks of an emigrant 'coffin ship' and was all too often a ticket to a burial at sea.

Altogether a forbidding picture of life in the less fortunate of Disraeli's two nations. Yet, despite all the immense social difficulties of the time, and notwithstanding Peterloo, Merthyr, Tolpuddle and Rebecca and all the other manifestations of social violence and protest in the early nineteenth century, the revolution expected by many in Britain in the half century following the French experience was never more than a spectre. And all the more remarkable is the patriotism and loyalty of the 'lower orders' among the British people. In fact, joy overflowed in both nations when the Victorian Age dawned in June, 1837, with the proclamation of the young Victoria as Queen. It was met in Carmarthen with:

> . . . demonstrations of loyalty and attachment, and a procession was formed of members of the Town Council and leading inhabitants, preceded by the military and a band of music, walking through the principal streets, stopping at various places to read the proclamation, which act was followed by enthusiastic cheering.
>
> The procession, which had a very imposing effect, was under the superintendence of Mr. Hall, our Chief Police Officer.
>
> Long and Happily Live our Glorious Queen.

When she was crowned a year later, it seemed as if her ascent to the throne presaged a new era in which the burdens of the poor, the depressed state of trade and industry, and all the inequalities of society would, somehow, disappear under the surge of enthusiasm which accompanied its dawning. Those who remember the accession of Queen Elizabeth II in the dreary post-war 1950s will have experienced a similar exultation.

In Carmarthen, the Coronation celebrations united the townspeople, for that short time at least, in a way that nothing else could. Thursday the 28th of June, 1838:

> . . . was observed as a festival to commemorate the Coronation of Her Gracious Majesty by all classes of her subjects in this town.
>
> In the morning, the Mayor and Body Corporate, accompanied by the clergy in canonicals, went in procession to Saint Peter's Church in this town, preceded by a band of music and the Staff of the Carmarthen Militia.
>
> Then followed the pensioners,[17] who met at Picton's Monument out of respect for that noble hero who fell at Waterloo, and on their return they marched through all the principal streets. They repaired to the 'Smith's Arms', Lammas Street, kept by a pensioner's widow with a large family of small children, where after the usual military ceremony on such occasions was gone

through, they entered and refreshed themselves with Cwrw Da, &c., and talked over some of the old hardships encountered—and 'Fought their battles o'er again.'

The following was the order of procession: Drum Major Richard Evans (ex-55th Regiment) in his uniform; fifes; some of the drummers in their uniforms; colours; banners; medals and other trophies of their service &c.

One of the colours was carried by Thomas Jones, who, with the 1st Regiment of Foot, lost his leg from the hip by entering a breach in the storming of Salamanca.[18]

The different pensioners by files, in number about fifty, appointed Sergeant Thomas Lewis, now engineer in the Carmarthen Gas Company, to be their commander, who conducted the business to their entire satisfaction.

All were proud to say that they had met together to demonstrate their respect for their Sovereign, Queen Victoria.

In the afternoon, the children from the different dissenting Sunday Schools in this town, amounting to several thousands, paraded the streets accompanied by their teachers, after which they repaired to a field in the vicinity of Water Street, where they were addressed by the Revs. Messrs. Worth and Watkins.

In the evening, there was a spontaneous illumination of the whole town, which was one perfect blaze of light.

The children of the schools connected with the established Church were regaled with tea in the evening in the school-room on the Parade.

Upon no former occasion was there a more unanimous and general display of sound loyalty and good feeling than was manifested by all ranks on this occasion.

This account throws an interesting sidelight on the growing influence in Carmarthen of the 'Sunday School' and the Church School, institutions which did more than anything else in those years before free, compulsory education[19] to lift the new generation from the pit of ignorance and to light the way to a better future for the generations to come. It is a debt which tends to be forgotten in these easier, affluent times, when man in his material security seems to have less need of his church.

Even so, life in the 1830s and 1840s was still dominated by rigid class divisions and those who had and those who had not might have been a thousand miles apart. Consider the contrasts between the town's glittering social occasions and, only yards away, the wretched lives of the starving poor.

Then, as now, the winter season saw the climax of the social calendar. There was for instance the Regimental Ball of the 1st King's Dragoon Guards who were stationed in the town in 1846. At the Boar's Head in Lammas Street, the officers and their "select company of ladies and gentlemen" danced right through the night in a whirl of waltzes and polkas, while champagne sparkled and wine flowed. The Carmarthen Hunt Ball:

> . . . which had been so anxiously looked forward to for many weeks by the grave and the gay, as a delightful reunion, came off at the Boar's head with an éclat surpassing any of the festive gatherings of the season, and amid the rapturous whirl of the dance the weather was forgotten.
>
> The company began to arrive at about half past ten o'clock and the carriages rapidly drew up in succession until 12 o'clock, when nearly the whole of the festive party had arrived. There were about eighty present, among whom were Colonel and Mrs. Love,[20] Colonel and Mrs. Browne, Captain Pinkney, the officers of the 13th Light Dragoons, the officers of the 41st Regiment, D. J. B. Edwards Esquire, of Rhydygorse, R. Hughes and G. Hughes Esquires, and Miss Hughes, Tregib, and the Misses Phillips, Aberglasny, (and so on). There were also several of the aristocracy of Glamorganshire present.
>
> When the whole of the party had assembled and when the ball had fairly commenced, the scene was one of the most brilliant and dazzling imaginable. The fair, the fashionable and the titled there assembled vied with each other and with the amenities of the ballroom. The polka, waltzes and quadrilles were danced during the night with little intermission. The polka was the favourite and all the tantalising gyrations of that fashionable dance were gone through with a dexterity and precision that left nothing to be wished for, but a longer night to enjoy it.
>
> Morning, however, dawned on the revellers and still found them at the polka.

But the winter (which "amid the rapturous whirl of the dance was forgotten") was exceedingly hard for the labouring poor, crammed into their tiny hovels on the Quay, on the Towyside and in the narrow back streets of the town. Their 'betters' still responded charitably every year, and relief was needed for "hundreds of poor families" in Carmarthen in the winter of 1837/38, in which:

Fahrenheit's thermometer indicated four degrees, or twenty-eight degrees below the freezing point on Friday morning the 19th of January at a quarter before nine o'clock.

Committees were formed:

. . . for the purpose of visiting the poor in order to ascertain who is in distress and what aid is most needed. The Committees will afford relief in coals, meat and flour at their discretion. It was proposed by Doctor Lawrence, and seconded by James Evans Esquire, Barrister, that a dispensary[21] should be established in this town.

Throughout the 1840s the story was the same. There were references to "the numerous poor of this town"; to "the fever that has been for some weeks past rather prevalent among the poorer classes of the town"; to "much local destitution and wretchedness"; and to "the accumulation of dirt in Water Street and the very neglected state of St. Catherine's Street and Goose Street, where sixteen persons were ill in one street, and one lying dead".[22] A particularly harrowing account of the living conditions of the poor was given at an inquest on a woman who had died of exposure in the snow:

An Inquest was held at the 'King's Arms', Priory Street, before George Thomas Jnr. Esquire,[23] on the body of Anne Rees, the wife of Rees Rees, a carpenter. After the jury had been sworn they proceeded to view the body, which had been removed to the house[24] where the deceased resided, and here a most wretched picture of misery presented itself. Five small children were grouped around the fireside with scarcely any clothing to cover them, and not a single article of furniture in the house, but of the most miserable kind.

The body of the deceased was crouched up, the arms perfectly rigid and placed across the forehead. At a short distance from the forehead there was a slight scar on the cheek, apparently caused by frost.

So bad was the weather that the man who found her body told the Coroner that "It was not a fit night for any Christian to be out, dead or alive."

That winter (of 1846) was the worst for many years, and snow isolated the town:

The roads have become almost impassable and the mails to

Pembrokeshire and Cardigan have been obliged to discontinue their journeys. Travelling is almost entirely suspended, as the snow is so immensely thick on the roads that the horses are almost buried in it.

It was indeed hard on the poor, and poverty in overcrowded hovels was bad enough, but Carmarthen still had big problems with the condition of its streets and its townspeople's lack of appreciation of the need for hygiene and sanitation, a trait which frequently brought epidemic and death to their town. Many people kept pigs in their yards and the animals wandered at will in large numbers around streets amply provided with rubbish for them to feed on. The narrow streets were made almost impassable by parked carts and waggons, piles of builders material and debris, and mounds of dung, ashes and dirt, prompting letters like one to the Editor of the *Carmarthen Journal* which complained that:

The practice of throwing ashes and filth in the public streets is what would not be allowed by a well-regulated community. Yours &c. A Ratepayer.

and one that suggested:

Were the present police but to do their duty by clearing the streets of nuisances, particularly pigs, they would deserve the thanks of the town. Yours &c. A Heavy Ratepayer.

N.B. Since writing this letter, I find to my surprise that two additional policemen were sworn in this day . . . what a shame!

Even when, in the 1840s, the Council employed "scavengers" with carts to keep down the accumulations of rubbish in the streets, most people saw it as a licence to throw out more than ever, prompting another letter:

Now the ashes, sweepings and even the manure from the stables are ranged openly in large heaps in the most frequented thoroughfares, as may be witnessed every day in Queen Street &c., to the evident disgust of persons passing through and with the evident risk of upsetting the mailcoach and other carriages. A few dozen urchins may be seen diverting themselves every morning by jumping in leap-frog fashion over the heaps, seeming to be moved by that good old maxim that manure does no good until it is spread.

I have myself seen several of the magistrates of the borough

> compelled to stop on their way up the Parade to wait women to finish riddling ashes before a double set of hovels called Parade Row, which, by the way, is one of the dirtiest thoroughfares in town, especially on Sundays, when the inhabitants make it a practice to throw out their ashes, cockles, mussels and oyster shells, and also empty 'certain' utensils there late on Saturday nights. Yours &c. A Ratepayer.

And there were other problems in the town, for Carmarthen's traders were feeling the effects of the national economic depression of the time, to which even the best established businesses fell victim, and the reverberations were felt through all classes of the townspeople. Under the heading "Depression of Trade at Carmarthen", the *Carmarthen Journal* expressed regret at:

> . . . having to mention the greatly depressed state of the trade in this town. We are given to understand that Mr. Owen Jones, draper of this place, has been appointed by the creditors of Mr. John Llewellyn, Blue Street, a bankrupt, to dispose of Mr. Llewellyn's very extensive stock at half the original cost, in order to produce an early dividend.
>
> We are sorry to say that this sale is likely to prove highly injurious to the regular trade.

The bankrupt Mr. Llewellyn's business had originally been Morley's, Carmarthen's celebrated cabinet makers, the site of whose former extensive works is commemorated to-day in the name of Morley Street, behind Lammas Street. The size and variety of the stock described in the advertisement of the sale, and the high standing of the collapsed firm, testify to the severity of the economic winter of 1837/1838.

As to the working conditions in shops like John Llewellyn's, the relationship between master and servant, and the discipline under which the latter were held may be judged by the positively Dickensian tone of the report in February, 1839, that shopkeepers in the town had acceded to a request from their assistants and apprentices that the shops should close at eight o'clock at night instead of nine. But the report warned that:

> . . . the continuation of such a system will depend much upon the conduct of the assistants and apprentices. If the extra time afforded to them[25] is profitably employed, the masters will rejoice in having agreed to their request, but on the other hand, should

the additional hours be spent licentiously, nothing will remain to be done but to revert to the former practice.

And when (in 1846) yet another hour was knocked off the working day, by closing at eight o'clock in the summer months as well, it was seen as ". . . testifying to the interest the employers take in the welfare of their assistants", who were exhorted to ". . . show to their employers that they are not unmindful or ungrateful for the favour". They could do this by:

> . . . showing how much they appreciate the advantage by becoming members of the mechanics' institution[26] by which means they may acquire a store of useful knowledge and make them wiser and better members of society.

The efforts of workers to organise themselves and to escape from this paternalistic attitude towards working hours and conditions led to a great deal of unrest and violence around the country, though Carmarthen was mercifully free of it. For all that, employers in Carmarthen still had recourse to the magistrates' court in dealing with disobedient employees. In May, 1837, for example:

> At the Guildhall, before the Mayor and E. H. Stacey, Esquire, Magistrates, William Edmunds, a workman at the tinworks of this town, charged with having absconded himself from the employ of Messrs. Downman and Company, not having given proper notice, was sentenced to one month's imprisonment.

NOTES

[1] *The Town Labourer 1760-1832,* J. L. Hammond and Barbara Hammond (Longmans, London, 1932).

[2] Nicholson's *History of the English Corn Laws,* quoted in *The Town Labourer,* op. cit.

[3] A 4lb. joint of beef of average quality would have taken the whole of a labourer's weekly wage. Furthermore, tea and coffee were taken only by the well-to-do, and the labourer's whole weekly wage would have purchased either a ½lb. of tea or 3lbs. of coffee. At dirt-cheap prices, ale and gin were the staple drinks of the 'lower orders' with the inevitable consequences.

[4] The twelve-pillared market hall (removed in 1846 when the present market site was laid out) stood where General Nott's monument now stands, above the Guildhall.

[5] "Our Sovereign Lord the King Chargeth and Commandeth all persons being assembled immediately to disperse themselves and peaceably to depart to their habitations or to their lawful business, upon the pains [sentence of death!] contained in

the Act made in the first year of King George the First for preventing tumults and riotous assemblies. God Save the King."

[6]In 1831, at the time of the agitation for electoral reform, a mere 3% or so of the population of England and Wales had the vote. To-day the figure is about 73%.

[7]*The Duke,* Philip Guedalla (Hodder & Stoughton Ltd., London, 1931).

[8]For which read 'English, Welsh, Scots and Irish'. The all-embracing term of the day was 'English'.

[9]The words of Sir Samuel Romilly, whose campaign against such widespread use of the death penalty ended with his suicide in 1818. (*The 19th Century: A History,* Robert Mackenzie, T. Nelson & Sons, London, 1882).

[10]The Baptist congregation moved over from their meeting house in Red Street, which was taken over by the Unitarians and, later, the Quakers.

[11]On the site of its direct descendant, the present Ivy Bush Royal Hotel.

[12]See *A Shilling for Carmarthen.*

[13]Only the Boar's Head is left now, near the bottom end of Lammas Street.

[14]At Alltycnap, on the western edge of the Borough.

[15]The first Factory Act was passed in 1833 to reduce the working day of children between 9 and 13 to a maximum of 8 hours, from the previous maximum of 12. The working week of young people between 13 and 18 years was thenceforth not to exceed sixty-nine hours!

[16]In 1830 an American visitor to Britain wrote that "The term pauper as used in England and more particularly in agricultural districts, embraces the numerous class of society who depend for subsistence solely upon the labour of their hands."

[17]Time-expired soldiers who were liable for call-out as a reserve. They were 'out-patients' of the Royal Hospital, Chelsea; many were well over the age of sixty and most had fought in Wellington's campaigns. See *A Shilling for Carmarthen* for their experiences in the Rebecca Riots.

[18]22nd July, 1812, during Wellington's Peninsular campaigns.

[19]Enacted in 1870.

[20]The District Army Commander.

[21]Carmarthen had no proper hospital until 1846, when the Priory Street Infirmary was opened.

[22]All quoted from the *Carmarthen Journal.*

[23]Son of George Thomas, of "Reform" election riot notoriety.

[24]Between the Parade and the tin works further along the riverside.

[25]A 12-hour instead of a 13-hour day.

[26]The word 'mechanic' was used in the sense of 'workman'; thus it referred to a workers' educational institute.

## ARRIVALS

As the nineteenth century reached its half-way mark, Carmarthen was touched by two external events, whose effect was aggravated by a longstanding local condition. The potato famine in Ireland in the late 1840s decimated that country's population by death and emigration[1] and swarms of destitute and starving peasants crossed the Irish Sea to Wales. The arrival of hundreds of them in Carmarthen coincided with the westward march of the deadly cholera plague, to meet in Carmarthen's still filthy and unhygienic back streets and hovels. It was a meeting whose consequences would be far reaching. The death and misery which came with it led to a previously unknown appreciation in Carmarthen (and, indeed, throughout the country) of the need for social hygiene . . . in its way as much a turning point as the coming of the railway.

The ancestors of many of Carmarthen's present-day townspeople were among the pitiful bands of gaunt-faced, ragged paupers whose arrival was graphically described by the *Carmarthen Journal* in April, 1848:

> The influx of the 'finest peasantry' into this town during the present week has been immense. On Sunday night last, no less than sixty three were admitted into the Workhouse, and having been supplied with supper, lodging and breakfast, were the next morning sent out of town by the Police, though we believe many, if not all, found their way back by night.
>
> They were landed from a vessel which arrived at Milford last week, the captain of which had first intended to disembark them at Newport, Monmouthshire, but finding that the authorities of that place would reship them for Ireland, he made for Milford and there landed his motley crew in a state of great destitution, as when searched at the workhouse, only twopence was found among the whole lot.
>
> On Wednesday night another batch, consisting of above thirty, were admitted into the Workhouse. This is now getting a very serious evil and some stop should be at once put to it.

And a year later, as the potato blight raged again through Ireland:

> The town this week has been literally swarming with Irish vagrants who were landed at Milford or some part of the coast in the neighbourhood early in the week, and who to the number of about four hundred of men, women and children have appeared in crowds in the streets. They say that the Parish Officers [in Ireland] paid two shillings a head for their passage to this country.
>
> Surely the government ought to adopt some measures to prevent such wholesale migration. The inhabitants of this country are sufficiently burdened with the support of their own poor without having such hordes as these to be a continual burden upon them.

And three years on they were still pouring into west Wales. Early in 1852:

> A vessel called the 'Catherine', of which a man named Murray is the master, arrived at Llanelli from one of the ports of Ireland, bringing a cargo of about one hundred and fifty wretched, hungry and tattered inhabitants of the 'Emerald Isle'. These poor creatures, consisting of men, women and children, pay fares averaging from a shilling [5p] to two shillings [10p] each for their passage from Ireland, the master engaging to land them at his port of destination, from whence they scatter themselves over the already over-burdened Unions of Wales, spreading wretchedness, squalor and filth wherever they go.

The Irish peasantry were looked upon as savages, and their tribulations were seen by most with the detachment of people today reading of famine or natural disaster among remote tribes in Africa. A *Carmarthen Journal* Editorial in August, 1848, voiced the contemporary attitude towards their fate:

> It is very strange that while the Irishman at home is idle, dirty, discontented and bloodthirsty, take him away from the vaunted 'Green Isle' and he appears to become a different being.
>
> In London and in the English provinces the hardest working labourers are Irishmen. Ask railway contractors what class of labourers they prefer for their heavy earthworks and they will tell you Irishmen.
>
> There is every reason and encouragement, therefore, to transplant the lazy, apathetic watcher of his miserable potato plot to another soil.

The arrival of these 'hordes' in Carmarthen added greatly to the congestion in the poorer parts of the town, particularly along the riverside in Dan y Banc and Kidwelly-fach, where many of them settled. As they found cottages there, they pressed more and more of their fellow immigrants into them, causing the town authorities—fearful of the epidemics which would undoubtedly follow—to clamp down on "unregistered lodging houses". John Sullivan was one of dozens brought before the magistrates, and his case fairly illustrates the magnitude of the problem. Police Constable Jones told the Court that:

> He went into the defendant's house, situated in Kidwelly-fach,

> where he found thirteen persons, men, women and children, in one small room. Some of them were gone to bed and others were preparing to follow their example. There were several others outside of the house waiting for them to depart, when they, too, would have gone in.
>
> In reply to the Mayor, Mr. Kentish (prosecuting)[2] said defendant's house was considered unfit in every respect for lodgers, and therefore the magistrates had refused to register it. Its dimensions were twelve feet square by seven feet high. The occupier himself had eight children.
>
> Mr. Kentish denominated Kidwelly-fach 'A little Irish Colony', and requested that something might be done to abate the nuisance.

Inevitably, this influx did nothing at all to improve the hygiene of the town, which suddenly assumed an unaccustomed importance as the frightened townspeople contemplated the approach of cholera across England in 1848. Carmarthen had already experienced an outbreak of smallpox only a year before, when it was reported that:

> The fearful spread of the Smallpox in this town is now chiefly confined to the lower classes, and in many cases terminating fatally.

The first stirrings of the cholera scare came in a letter to the Editor of the *Carmarthen Journal* in August, 1848:

> Sir, the rapid and certain approach westwards of that fateful scourge the cholera makes it an imperative duty not only on the authorities of towns, but on the overseers and officials of County Parishes likewise to effect the immediate removal of stagnant drains, to prevent the accumulation of dirt in front of houses and to cause the cottages of the poor to be washed with lime.
>
> If we cannot arrest the progress of this fearful disease, still it may be possible to modify its effects by stopping contagion.

This letter was written while the cholera was still confined to the Continent, though marching relentlessly westward and leaving many thousands dead. But two months later, in a long editorial (in the *Carmarthen Journal*), the shocked townspeople read that:

> The Asiatic Cholera has at length made its way to this country. On its former visitation [in 1839] it came from Hamburg to Sunderland and it appears to have done so now. Subsequently the

disease has appeared among the convicts at Woolwich[3] and finally in London itself, so there no longer remains any doubt of the fact.

Epidemics delight in filth and foul air. The chief predisposing causes of every epidemic, especially of Cholera, are damp, moisture, filth and animal and vegetable matter in a state of decomposition. Attacks of Cholera are found uniformly to be most frequent and virulent in low-lying districts, on the banks of rivers, in the neighbourhood of sewer mouths and wherever there are large collections of refuse, particularly amidst human dwellings.

Carmarthen fitted this formula perfectly! In fact, the editorial concluded with a few examples:

> It will be conceded that there is a deficiency of sanitary arrangements in Carmarthen. We need only advert to the abominations which will meet the eye of those who visit the courts, alleys and passages in various parts of the town. We find that the houses in one of the chief entrances to the town, Priory street, have drains running through them, which together with a pig-sty here and there empty their contents into the public streets.

Fear brought action. On Friday the 13th of October, 1848:

> . . . a meeting of members of the medical profession in this town was held at the Town Hall to take into consideration the best means of ascertaining the state of the ventilation, drainage and cleanliness of the town, so as to stay the progress of the Cholera should it unhappily reach this town. There were present J. Bowen, M.D., H. Lawrence, M.D., J. Jenkins, E. H. Stacey, W. James, J. Hughes and J. Rolands, Esquires.
>
> In the event of the Cholera invading the town, as they all well knew, they had no place to put the patients, and it would be well to get some places provided so that the poor might be removed thereto as soon as attacked. It was true the Board of Health in London had recommended that the patients should be left in their own habitations, but in a town like this, where five or six families occupied one house, each family consisting of five or six persons, with only one bed and blanket for the whole family, the best plan next to providing a place for the whole family would be to remove the patient.

The committee considered the wards of the Workhouse as a temporary expedient, but they were to encounter insurmountable objections. They did, however, succeed in making arrangements for a survey of the condition of the town, dividing it into eight districts for inspection by the medical men.

A fortnight later, the Town Council met, and:

> Dr. Bowen reported that the state of the town as regarded ventilation [of buildings], cleanliness and draining was very deplorable, particularly in regard to necessaries [lavatories], there being many houses without any. The drainage was also very bad and some of the houses were very much crowded, in many instances, there being in single rooms six, seven or eight persons with only one bed amongst the whole number, and in many instances not more than two blankets.
>
> If this town were to be visited by the Cholera, it would certainly attack families in that condition, who would be occupying the same bed and only one pair of blankets amongst the whole.
>
> The first thing to be attended to was the draining of the town, and all the funds that could be spared ought to be devoted to that purpose. They ought also to remove the dunghills and ash pits that existed in the town, and which were made the receptacles for all kinds of filth.
>
> Another evil that required to be remedied was the want of necessaries [lavatories]. On the left side of Picton Terrace there was hardly one to be found. There were not more than six or eight at the outside, and some of them were in a filthy state.

There is nothing like the spectre of death to concentrate the mind.

In a flurry of activity in the town generally, the magistrates' court was busy issuing summonses against those failing to abate "nuisances":

> On November 3rd, before the Mayor and E. H. Stacey and William Morris Esquires [Magistrates], Mr. Collard, the Town Surveyor, reported that a dead horse had been placed under one of the arches at Kidwelly-fach by Mr. Children. It was getting into a putrid state and as it was a case of emergency he applied for a summons without the usual notice.
>
> Mr. W. Morris stated that the stench arising from Kidwelly-fach at times was most offensive, and quite sufficient of itself to create infection. He had been informed that Mr. Children fed his pigs with the entrails of dead horses and stinking fish, and the stench arising from these being deposited there was most injurious. Summonses in this case were granted.

Even the wandering pigs of the town were brought under control by the police and the magistrates:

> John Evans, who is popularly known by the designation 'Old Offender' was summoned to answer the complaint of P.C. Miles Davies for allowing his 'Old Sow' to wander through the streets.
>
> The defendant's wife [after a fine had been inflicted] said she would endeavour to sell the 'Old Sow' at the next market day, and thus effectively keep the poor beast out of the fangs of the police.

Providentially, the cholera did not reach Wales in 1848, but in June of the following year the people of Carmarthen heard the dreaded news that portended the death of many of them:

> The Cholera at Cardiff: This dreadful scourge has made its devastating appearance in Cardiff. There have been from sixty to seventy cases in the town within the last fortnight, a very considerable number of which have terminated fatally.
>
> Cholera at Merthyr: Several fresh cases took place on Monday and proved fatal, but on the whole it appears that it has rather abated otherwise. Lime is given at the police station to all who are too poor to purchase it, for the purpose of lime-washing their homes.

During the next fortnight, Carmarthen magistrates' court was full of 'filth' cases as frantic efforts were made to cleanse the town . . . and the cholera moved nearer and nearer. It was at Brecon by the 26th of June, when it was reported that of seven hundred and forty-six cases (in three weeks), three hundred and seven had terminated fatally. In Merthyr, in the midst of "the most assiduous efforts to promote cleanliness", about one hundred and forty died, out of two hundred and seventy four cases.

Meanwhile, sweeping recommendations were being made to the Town Council by Carmarthen's Public Health Inspector, who reported that the normal mortality rate in the town was as high as 26.2 in the thousand,[4] "a figure above the rate fixed by the legislature as justifying interference on behalf of the poor". And he painted a daunting picture of Carmarthen, saying that:

> . . . the whole of the town is remarkably ill-provided with privvies and is on this account in a very filthy state, which is rendered worse by the presence of foul, open ditches in the suburbs.

Burial grounds in the town—including that of Saint Peter's Church—were over crowded and becoming a danger to public health, a fact which persuaded the Home Office to order the closure of three of them and the commencement of a new burial ground away from the town's habitations. The new burial ground, near Trevaughan Village, was opened in 1856 and is in use to this day.

On the very day the Public Health Inspector reported, the cholera struck

> . . . first in an Alley near the Guildhall, known by the name of Spurrell's yard, where no less than four cases have terminated fatally, some of the unfortunate creatures not having had the benefit of medical advice, as the guardians in the exercise of their discretion saw fit to dismiss the additional medical men appointed only twelve days before. For the sake of a few paltry pounds, they jeopardise the lives of their fellow creatures.

For the next three months the disease raged through the narrow streets, the lanes and the courts which comprised the poor quarters of the town, carrying off a total of one hundred and two people out of three hundred and fifty-four known cases. The "medical men" worked valiantly, and there can be no doubt that despite administrative problems and petty squabbling, a good deal of cleaning up had been accomplished in the time which Carmarthen's geographical position had allowed.

Of a total death toll of over fifty-three thousand in England and Wales, Carmarthen's contribution was far less than it might otherwise have been.

This particular cholera epidemic was a traumatic national experience, and lessons had been learned, because the mid-nineteenth century saw the arrival of the concept of 'Social Medicine' as the basis for public health legislation. Beginning with efforts to purify London's water supply, the government went on to legislate for other measures recommended by the English public health reformer Edwin Chadwick, in his report of 1842—municipal water supplies, scientific drainage, and an independent public health service with powers to deal with those who endangered the lives of others by pollution or 'nuisances', for which only ineffectual by-laws had hitherto been available. Chadwick also proposed a service for the interment of the dead, since bodies often remained for days in the overcrowded homes of the poor.

A watershed indeed, but such enlightenment was slow to reach Carmarthen . . . more than thirty years slow. The cholera visitation of 1866 carried off fifty-four people, against a total death toll in England and Wales of twenty thousand, and poverty and lowly conditions were to be the lot of the poor people of the town for many decades yet.

If the authorities in the town had been sadly lacking in not attending to its sanitary deficiencies, the same cannot be said of their approach to the town's structural development, and the markets were the prime example in a spate of public building. In 1846 they were removed from their centuries old home above and around the Guildhall to a commodious new area on the reclaimed ground of the old Wide Ocean. The end of the old markets came when:

> The materials of the Old Cross and Cheese Market[5] were sold by auction on Monday the 27th of July, 1846 and fetched the respective prices of £7.10s.0d. [£7.50p] and £5. One relic has alone been preserved from the general ruin and deposited in safe custody: the stocks, the 'terror of all drunken and disorderly persons'.

The arrival of the new markets was signalled by the announcement that:

> The workmen and labourers engaged on the building—amounting to about 120 in number—will, we understand, be plentifully regaled with the 'Good Fare of Old England'—roast beef and plum pudding, with a sufficient quantity of Cwrw Da to liquify the solids—this evening at six o'clock in the Market Place, preparatory to its opening tomorrow [Saturday the 1st of August, 1846].

And so the big day arrived, and the *Carmarthen Journal* report of the opening of the new markets conveys the flavour of the wholesale transfer of all the market activity and its attendant bustle from its time-honoured home in the cramped town centre to its new one, proudly described as:

> . . . a very handsome one, which will bear comparison with any in the Kingdom. We are not merely expressing our own opinion,

Going to market. *(National Library of Wales).*

but that of all who have visited it, and those number not a few from every part of the Kingdom.

It's opening was a huge success, and it was found that there was:

> . . . no difficulty in getting the country people to go in with their produce. The streets, which usually on a market day are one continued scene of bustle and excitement, were comparatively deserted, and everything outside the market walls wore a most quiet appearance.
>
> Not so inside: the place being crowded throughout the day with persons of all classes, most of whom made some purchases—a great many for the novelty of the thing.
>
> Jewellery and jam-tarts, cakes and cutlery, perfumery and potatoes, greengrocery and gloves, pins and pots, cabbages and corkscrews, timepieces and taffies, tea-kettles and toothbrushes, confectionery and coffee pots, lolipops and leather, flannel and fish, cheese and crockery, hats and handkerchiefs—with a hundred other etceteras—were spread out in the most alluring forms to tempt the spectators to become purchasers.
>
> Mr. Collard, the Clerk of the Market, was present and did his duty most efficiently. Some fish that were not quite so fresh as they might be were condemned and sent out of the market.

Some of the prices of the time in Carmarthen Market illustrate the increasing availability of wholesome food to the labouring classes: Wheat (40 lbs.) 5s.8½d (29p); Barley (40 lbs.) 3s.8d (18½p); Oats (40 lbs.) 2s.2¾d (11½p); Beef, fourpence (just over 1½p) a pound; Mutton, fivepence (about 2p) a pound; Veal, fourpence a pound; Pork, fivepence a pound; Butter, eightpence (3½p) a pound; Turkeys, three shillings (15p) each; Geese, 3s.6d (17½p) each; Ducks, 1s.6d (7½p) each; "Fowls", ninepence (nearly 4p) each; Cheese, 15s.0d (75p) per hundredweight; Eggs, nine for sixpence (2½p); Potatoes, 8 lbs. for three pence (about 1p).

The markets were (and still are) the heart of Carmarthen's commercial life, and the construction of their new home was the major project in a busy period of town development, for Carmarthen, like the nation as a whole, was emerging from economic depression into the period of expansion and pros-

The market clock tower preserved—before and after. *(National Library of Wales). (Pat Molloy).*

perity that was to characterise the Victorian Age. For evidence of the quality and durability of the facilities provided in the new market, we need look no further than the fact that it was not until nearly a hundred and forty years later that any major change was looked for. In 1981, a completely rebuilt provision market was opened on the same site, the only remaining relic of the 1846 market being the clock tower, refurbished and used as centre-piece at the front of the large new open market hall. Happily, the design of the new market hall and the layout of the stall area outside preserved all of the distinctive atmosphere for which the old Carmarthen Market was so widely known.

The middle years of the century also saw the provision (across Saint Catherine's Street from the new market) of a new slaughterhouse and cattle market that was also to serve the town for well over a century. It contained:

> . . . accommodation for slaughtering 100 beasts, 300 sheep, 300 calves and 150 pigs, and the new Cattle Market will be large enough to accommodate 3,000 sheep in pens, 2,000 pigs in pens, 500 head of cattle and 100 horses, the remainder of the land to be left for the exhibition of shows &c.

Proof indeed of the burgeoning agricultural economy of the district, to which the Carmarthen Farmers' Club, formed in the early 1850s, added its own impetus by encouraging the use of the newest farming practices and techniques.

The town's educational and cultural ambitions were looked to by a committee chaired by the Mayor, which raised a subscription to erect a large and sumptuously furnished building containing 'Public Rooms', in King Street:

> . . . suitable to the requirements of the town, for the purposes of a Literary and Scientific Institution, Assemblies, Concerts, &c.—a combination of Instruction and Amusement.

We see in this period, too, significant developments in education and religion in the town. Carmarthen's private schools continued to provide lessons—of varying quality—to the children of the fee paying middle class, and the endowed grammar schools continued to cater for the further education of the brighter of them. At Sir Thomas Powell's Endowed Grammar School in 1852 the terms varied from thirty Guineas (£31.50) per year for boarders. For day scholars under ten

Carmarthen, in the middle of the nineteenth century. *(Carmarthen Museum).*

years, the fee was six Guineas (£6.30) and for those above ten, eight Guineas (£8.40). The courses there embraced "Religious instruction in conformity with the principles of the Established church, the classics, mathematics, general history, geography and mapping, geometry, algebra, mensuration, book-keeping, arithmetic, English grammar and composition". The advertisement explained that:

> The terms include everything, so that the parent knows exactly what he has to pay. Music, French, Drawing and Dancing if required. Each boarder has a separate bed. A library is provided for the use of the pupils. Strict regard is required to punctuality.

Miss Emily Saunders' Spilman Street Academy of Dancing and Deportment provided "lessons in the Polka, the Valse à deux temps &c.", and the Misses Morris in Lammas Street provided a genteel education for the young ladies of the better-off Carmarthen families. At the Presbyterian College, for nine Guineas [£9.45], lay students could study in the Theological Department under the Reverend Davies, in the Classical and Mathematical Department under Doctor Lloyd, and in the Department of Modern and Oriental Languages under Doctor Davison.

The two new 'Lancastrian' schools,[6] one for boys and one for girls, provided a basic 'Three Rs' education for the children of those of the poor people of the town who were prepared to forego the pennies their children could otherwise have earned. Financed by charitable institutions, they showed the need, and paved the way, for free and compulsory education for the masses, which was still nearly thirty years away. The strides made over the first half of the century were quite remarkable given the small contribution made by central government—as little as £30,000 in 1839. By about 1850 this independent system had increased the number of public and private schools in England and Wales from 3,500 at the turn of the century to 45,000 by 1850, and doubled the proportion of the country's children receiving education.

Carmarthen was in the forefront of this educational explosion, its new Teacher Training College producing the first trained teachers for the Welsh charity schools system. In June, 1853, it was announced that:

The Carmarthen Teacher Training College, 1853. *(National Library of Wales).*

> The Welsh Education Committee have during the past year continued their superintendence of the Training Institution at Carmarthen, of which the Reverend W. Reed is still the Principal. Several schools in the Principality have now been supplied with masters trained at Carmarthen, and the Committee have reason to believe that they have been found well qualified for their work.

Right through the century Carmarthen celebrated any Royal occasion with an enthusiasm second to none, and each succeeding occasion carried with it evidence of the way in which the gulf between Disraeli's "two nations" was narrowing. The duty diary of Sergeant David Williams (a member of the Carmarthen Borough Police Force when, in 1857, it reached a strength of twelve men and became the legendary 'Carmarthen Shilling'[7]) contains an entry relating to one such Royal occasion, with a brevity that gives scant indication of its dimensions:

> Tuesday 10th March, 1863. I performed duty as follows from 8.30 a.m. to 1.45 p.m. at the boat racing, and assisted in the procession formed in celebration of the marriage of H.R.H. The Prince of Wales[8] round the town. From 2 till 5.30 p.m. at the Cattle Market and Mr. Norton's field while the rustic sports were going on. From 6 to 9 p.m. in Nott Square and Guildhall Square while the fireworks were going on, and from 9.30 until 11 p.m. at the Assembly Rooms.

Fourteen and a half hours duty. But it was a day of days.

> Tuesday (and a brighter day could not be wished) was ushered in about 6.30 a.m. with merry peals of the Church bells, together with firing of cannon, the latter of which not a little startled the inhabitants out of their night's repose. The Russian Trophy was conveyed from its resting place at the Fusilier Monument to the Pothouse[9] and at intervals during the day, under the control of a Sergeant of Artillery, uttered forth its warlike sounds, which would however be considered more loyal to the hearts than pleasing to the ears. Smaller cannon were also fired throughout the day.
>
> At 7 o'clock [in the morning] the Volunteer Drum and Fife Band played through the town, commencing at Picton's Monument. At nine o'clock old Carmarthen Bridge, the Quay and embankment presented a gay appearance, each place being thronged by thousands of persons all attired in holiday attire and decorated with a variety of descriptions of wedding favours, to witness several boatraces.
>
> The first was a coracle race from Carmarthen Bridge, round a boat moored off the Pothouse Quay and back to the Bridge. Eight coracles came to the scratch and on the signal being given off they went and kept together like a group of partridges, each man being quite at home in his one-oared boat. However, on their return the receding tide told the tale on these primitive little vessels and the strongest arm and muscle would best. The following were first at the winning post:
>
> William Thomas, Dan y Banc (first); Griffith Lewis, Dan y Banc (second); David Lewis, Dan y Banc (third) and William Lewis, Dan y Banc (fourth)—and all were loudly cheered.

The Lewises nearly swept the board in the next coracle race too, taking the first three places, with Samuel Evans of Parcyberllan and John Morris of Dan y Banc tieing for fourth place.

Other boat races delighted the cheering crowds, while Mr. Hillier, the manager of the Carmarthen and Cardigan Railway enlivened the proceedings with his own ''novel manifestation of loyalty''—the firing of twenty-one detonating signals under the wheels of the Mail Train!

And then, just before noon, the crowds surged from the riverside through Blue Street and Quay Street to the Guildhall Square to join the procession. The Carmarthen Volunteers and the Royal Carmarthenshire Artillery were paraded there and fired a volley into the air as the clock struck the hour. The military bands played the National Anthem, the "numerous choir" sang 'God Bless the Prince of Wales' (the newly composed masterpiece of Carmarthen's own Brinley Richards) and then, marshalled by Sergeant Major Kyle, the huge procession set off through Nott Square to walk all the principal streets of the town and to return to the Square down Lammas Street from Picton's Monument. As befitted a procession in a busy seaport, it was given a maritime flavour by a model of a ship borne in front by a sailor, who was followed by the British Ensign and Union Jack carried by river pilots, and eighteen ships' colours carried by river pilots and hobblers (quay labourers). The bands and the soldiers were followed by the students of the Teachers' Training College, the masters and boys of the endowed schools, the members of the town's masonic lodges, the inhabitants of the town four abreast and—symbolising the importance of the river—twenty coraclemen carrying their coracles in the traditional way, reminiscent of large black beetles, their heads hidden and their backs bowed under their black-tarred craft.

Things began to get out of hand, though, when the "rustic sports" began in the Market Place, where:

> . . . in consequence of the pressure and excitement of the mob the effect of all the fun anticipated was only a disorderly melee, in which everyone had to take care of himself to save being crushed to death.
>
> It was then determined to resume the sports in Mr. Norton's field, but on proceeding there the mob became more unruly still, so that matters got worse and the whole affair ended in complete failure.

Elsewhere in the town things were more orderly. The children of the National and St. David's Sunday Schools were entertained to lunch "by the kindly benevolence of Isaac Horton Esquire, High Sheriff of the County" who also gave a half-crown [12½p] each to twenty of the most aged poor of the town and "liberally supplied the prisoners in the County Gaol with a good dinner of meat and vegetables". The children of the National, Lancastrian and Saint Peter's Sunday Schools and the Roman Catholic school, and the paupers of the Workhouse were "regaled with a plentiful supply of tea and plum cake'', and the male inmates of the Workhouse were presented with an ounce of tobacco, while the female inmates each received half an ounce of snuff.

Throughout a town decorated with banners and garlands, fireworks crackled and bonfires burned and the day ended with the inevitable ball at the Assembly Rooms, which was somewhat marred by the fact that:

> Jones' Quadrille Band played a badly assorted variety of dance music in a manner very little to their credit. Suffice it to say that the only opinion that prevailed was that the music favoured by them was flimsy and slovenly to a degree.

Even so, dancing continued until four o'clock in the morning and the revellers must have been exhausted as they made their ways home through the gas lit streets in the darkness of that March morning under the bleary eyes of policemen who would not be able to sleep off their hangovers for several hours yet!

## NOTES

[1] Between 1845 and 1850 the 8 million population of Ireland was reduced to 6 million. Nearly a million died of starvation and a million more emigrated.

[2] Samuel Kentish was Chief Constable of the Carmarthen Borough Police Force from 1848 to 1870. It was he who first brought real order and discipline to the force.

[3] Awaiting transportation to Australia and confined in filthy, insanitary hulks, anchored in the River Thames.

[4] Nearly two and a half times greater than that for England and Wales in 1970.

[5] The site now of General Nott's monument in Nott Square.

[6] Named after the Quaker Joseph Lancaster (1778-1838) who devised a school system based on 'Monitors'—senior pupils who passed on their knowledge to their juniors, under the supervision of teachers who were thus able to supervise as many as a hundred pupils each.

[7] See *A Shilling for Carmarthen* for an account of David Williams' service and extracts from his duty diaries.

[8] The future King Edward the Seventh.

[9] A large storehouse at the lower end of the quay. The trophy was a large cannon captured in the Crimea.

## THE GULF NARROWS

The last thirty years of the nineteenth century were to see the last of the town's principal industries—weaving,[1] iron and tin —decline to the point of extinction. That century would then have seen Carmarthen succumb finally to the challenge of the industrial revolution and of the distance-shrinking revolution in transportation, to decline in status from the most populous and important town in Wales and the principal seaport of the south west of the Principality to an agricultural town of small, virtually static, population. It was a decline in status and fortune that brought with it many social problems, including unemployment, works closures and an exacerbation of the twin Carmarthen curses of poverty and drink, and of the seemingly insuperable health, sanitation and water-supply problems posed by the decay of the older and poorer sections of the town. Even so, Carmarthen was still an important and largely prosperous market town for a richly agricultural county, an asset which, in spite of all, guaranteed a stable future in a fast-changing world. But before that stable future was reached a good many people in the town would continue to experience much poverty and distress and the crowded soup kitchen for the poor would be a feature of the Carmarthen winter scene well beyond the century's end.

Winter always brought unimaginable hardships to a large proportion of the townspeople, and while the workhouse—always full to capacity—still provided relief for those who could repay it by "honest toil" in the shape, for example, of stone-breaking, there was little alternative to the soup kitchen for the young and infirm. The main Carmarthen soup kitchen and the smaller ones run independently by the churches and chapels, were supported by the charitable contributions of the better off, who always responded warmly to the frequent appeals by the Mayor for all manner of causes, from the all too common colliery disasters to such causes as the distress of the Lancashire cotton weavers thrown out of work by the Union blockade of Confederate cotton exports during the American civil war in the 1860s. Even the poor dug deep into their pockets for such appeals as these. In February, 1879, for example, while the distribution of soup and bread to hundreds of the Carmarthen poor was taking place in the Market Wool Room, funds were being collected in the town for the relief of the Welsh families left fatherless by the Zulu war.

The whole of Wales had been shocked by the news that 602 men of the 24th Regiment (The South Wales Borderers) were among the 1,445 Empire soldiers overwhelmed and slaughtered by 20,000 Zulus at Isandlwhana, a catastrophe only made bearable by the news of the heroic defence of nearby Rorke's Drift by a handful of men of that Regiment's 2nd Battalion. Prayers were offered in Saint Peter's and all the churches and chapels of Carmarthen, while the pounds and pennies collected from all classes of the townspeople were sent to the grief-stricken valleys of south Wales.

And in the Carmarthen Wool Room the work of charity went on:

> About 500 little ones partook of an excellent meal of soup and bread, and before commencing they sang 'Hold the Fort' and after dinner the exuberance of their delight found vent in 'Pull for the Shore' and 'Safe in the arms of Jesus'. The proceedings were superintended by Mrs. Thomas, Quay Street, Miss Jones, Wellfield, the Misses Warren, the ex-Mayor Mr. W. Morris, John Street, Mr. W. Jones, Long Acre Villa, Mr. Thomas Jeremy, Parcyvelvet School, Mr. Anthony, Commerce House, Mr. E. Colby Evans and several others.
>
> The arduous and continuous exertions made by the Chief Constable are worthy of special mention and the committee congratulate themselves on securing such an experienced and worthy coadjutor.
>
> On Monday last, after the children had all been satisfied, there remained a quantity of soup and bread. A number of decrepit men and women were brought into the Wool Room and the spare food set before them. Just as the second party were concluding, an old and infirm man came in. He was informed that the supply of bread was exhausted but that he might have soup. This he gratefully received and went round the tables gathering up the crumbs of bread left by the others.
>
> Care is taken that only those who need it shall partake of this charity. The town has been divided into districts which are regularly visited and the tickets sold at a penny each to the poor at their homes.

We see in that report an indication of the breadth of the contribution to the life of the town by the Borough Police—the 'Carmarthen Shilling'—who were as much involved in the relief of their fellow-townsmen's distress as in the curtailment of their excesses; indeed the old station house in Cambrian Place was often used as a supplementary soup kitchen. Few got as close as they did to the lives and homes and wretchedness of the poor.

There were other reasons than unemployment and loss of industries to account for the persistence of poverty in the town. One lay in the drift of the population from the rural areas to the new centres of industry, to the towns where the pavements were supposedly paved with gold. In twenty years, Carmarthen's population had remained more or less steady at ten thousand or so, but like most country towns in the early seventies the balance of its population had been disturbed through migration to the centres of industry. The departure of the young and strong to Eldorado had left behind a larger than normal proportion of the aged and very young, added to which —as a government health inspector had discovered—many of the emigrants returned, still young, worn out and diseased from their labours in mine, foundry and factory.

How else, for all the town's continuing sanitation problems, could the highest death-rate in the whole Kingdom be explained?

In the town of Carmarthen at the beginning of the 1870s the annual death-rate was a staggering 31.68 per thousand, as compared with the national average of only 22.4. And the difference between the statistics for the rural and urban areas of the borough told their own story about the conditions in the poorer parts of the town. In the rural areas the average age at death was thirty-nine years, while in the town it was only thirty-three. In England and Wales as a whole the average age at death was forty-one. The infant mortality rate in England was 12 per cent—in Carmarthen over 17 per cent. Thus, those born in the town who were lucky enough to survive their first year were then likely to die some six years before their country neighbours and some eight years earlier than those in England.

Only one in six in Carmarthen town died of old age![2]

Again contrary to the national picture, pauperism was on the increase, Carmarthen having three times the national average dependent on parish relief. 1,325 (or almost 13 per cent) of the townspeople were destitute, a situation so shocking that the town's Medical Officer of Health, Surgeon John Hughes, was moved to say "I hope that someone will be able to prove that these figures are wrong, as the conclusion arrived at from them seems to me to be incredible."[3] No one did.

Added to the imbalance in the population as a cause of this dreadful state of affairs was the continuing insanitary state of the town, its sewerage system only a little improved since the cholera visitation of 1849, following which a government inspector had made sweeping recommendations on the subject. Carmarthen was paying the price for its great age as a town; cesspools abounded among crowded buildings, which stood on land sodden with centuries of human waste. Many of the cesspools had remained unemptied for upwards of twenty years, the owners being "rather proud of the fact, as it saves the expense of emptying them, forgetting or ignoring that what saves them from some expense is often the cause of a poisonous nuisance to their neighbours".

Of the two larger parts of the town still undrained, that comprising Lammas Street, Goose Street, Upper and Lower Water Streets and Catherine Street were described by Dr. Hughes as having "crowded houses and a poor population living on a wet, cold and foul bed of clay saturated with human refuse". He warned the town's authorities about the potential for disease lurking in the ground, suggesting that:

> . . . any extensive works by which the surface soil would be much disturbed as in digging deep sewers should not be carried on during the hot summer months, and in an old town like this a very large portion of the work should not be done at the same time. There can be no doubt but that in the older parts of the town, where people have resided for centuries, the soil for a considerable depth must be saturated with organic refuse, and that their exposure to the air must be to a certain extent injurious to health. I would beg to remind you that when extensive works of the kind were going on in 1835 the town was visited by the severest epidemic of typhoid that had occurred for the last thirty years. Many persons were attacked in the course of three or four weeks and several died.

Even the new houses going up in Francis Terrace, Wellfield and Waun Dew had to have cesspools, so remote were they from the sewerage system, and to make matters worse they were in a part of the town that housed the municipal manure heaps—tons of horse manure, ashes, street sweepings and slaughterhouse offal. The heaps were sited there as the only alternative to the other—WINDWARD—side of town!

Only a third of all houses in Carmarthen were connected to the sewerage system, which had its outfalls on the river; a quarter of the houses had no lavatories and fewer than half were connected to the town's meagre water supply. But even these statistics and averages hid the real picture of overcrowding and poverty in the poor parts of the town. On the fashionable Parade, for example, 22 houses, with 72 bedrooms and 22 lavatories, housed 91 families. Below it, along Dan y Banc, 38 houses, with 36 bedrooms and only 7 lavatories, housed 128 families—or more than a dozen people to each bedroom!

Altogether a stark and forbidding picture of life and conditions in the 1870s. But as always not the whole picture. Carmarthen still had more than its share of problems, but it was still a busy, prosperous and lively market town in which most of its people could earn a living and find plenty of outlets for their traditional and undiminished boisterousness and capacity for enjoyment. As for living standards generally, wages in the town were outstripping prices and those in work could live reasonably well, though the improvidence and social ignorance which characterised many of the poorer classes still channelled much of their income into the town's innumerable alehouses. It would take such influences as free, compulsory education (enacted in 1870), the temperance movement of the eighties and nineties,[4] the religious revival of the turn of the century and the social upheavals accompanying the Great War of 1914-1918 to really get to the heart of that particular problem.

The tinworks of Thomas, Lester and Company at the end of Priory Street employed about 190 men and about 100 women and children, while the town's two iron foundries provided work for about 60 men and boys. The hat making trade, once one of the principal trades of the town, was, like the weaving trade, in steep decline, and many of those depending on it for a living were going through hard times. Carmarthen was an important centre for the printing trade and eight printing establishments gave employment to some sixty-five people. And there were still forty large families alongside the river

*Theo Rogers).*

Contrasts: The fashionable Parade, and Dan y Banc.

*(Carmarthen Museum).*

deriving an uncertain and precarious living from coracle fishing, supplemented by labouring jobs or river-dredging in the winter time.

It was in Carmarthen's character, though, that beer brewing and the hotel and pub trade provided a substantial proportion of the jobs in the town. Sixty people worked at the two breweries and the demand was such that expansion was called for:

> Monster Beer Vat at Messrs. Norton's Brewery: An enormous beer vat made by Mr. Oxley of Frome, Somersetshire, is now in course of erection at Messrs. Norton's Brewery, which measures forty one feet in circumference and is above twenty feet high. It is of an oval shape, and one may form some idea of its magnitude from the fact that when the vat is completed, the spirited proprietors propose giving a dinner to thirty of their principal workmen in the interior of it!

That "Monster Beer Vat" would help keep the glasses filled in the town's one hundred and seven hotels, inns and other licensed houses—one to every seventeen houses and one to every ninety-five inhabitants!

Wages were high and rising.[5] In the tinworks, hammermen could earn thirty-five shillings [£1.75p] a week, rollermen thirty-two shillings [£1.60p], "puddlers", refinery men and tinhouse men thirty-shillings [£1.50p] and labourers sixteen shillings and sixpence [82½p] a week. In the iron foundries, the smiths, moulders, fitters and pattern-makers earned twenty-five shillings [£1.25p], while weavers earned about £1, printing workers about twenty-two shillings [£1.10p], carpenters twenty-two shillings and sixpence [£1.12½p], plumbers thirty shillings [£1.50p] and painters twenty-four shillings [£1.20p]. The Chief Constable of the borough force was paid £100 a year, his sergeants twenty-six shillings [£1.30p] a week and his constables twenty-two shillings [£1.10p] a week.

And the cost of food? Beef, ninepence [4p] a pound, mutton tenpence [4p] a pound, butter tenpence a pound, potatoes three shillings [15p] a hundredweight, Welsh cheese twopence halfpenny [1p] a pound, and coal about a shilling [5p] a hundredweight. As a very rough measure of the cost of living, a 4 lb. joint of beef would cost a tin worker about nine per cent of his weekly wage. That was in 1873. In 1981, a man earning £100 a week would spend roughly the same proportion of his pay buying the same joint.

There was a wide range of entertainment and cultural activity in the town and no shortage of audiences for it. The chapels were flourishing, not only in their religious role but also in their contribution to moral uplift and education through the eloquence of visiting lecturers from far and wide, the most popular subjects being world travel and exploration illustrated by "magic lantern" slides. The Assembly Rooms in King Street, which contained the Literary and Scientific Institution, were also the venue for edifying lectures, as well as for choral, band and orchestral concerts and operas, performed by local amateurs and by professional touring companies. The open-air events—fairs, river regattas, the Guildhall Square band concerts, the race meetings—would always pull the crowds, and when a circus or menagerie came to town everyone turned out to watch the long procession wend its slow way through dense crowds come to cheer the splendidly scarlet-clad, gold-braided bandsmen, the tumblers, jugglers, clowns, cowboys and Indians, wildly dancing "Dervishes" and—favourite of all—the huge, gaudily painted, horse-drawn cages containing animals so wild and exotic as to astound people who had only seen their like in picture books. Even outside performance times they would draw crowds of curious onlookers, and never more so than when the elephants were led into the Towy at low water for exercise. An especially loud cheer went up the day one of the elephants tried to climb into a rowing boat and pushed it to the bottom! And when the nights drew in there were the weekly "Winter Evening Entertainments" of poetry and prose readings, songs, piano pieces and light orchestral items performed by local talent at the Guildhall and in the Assembly Rooms. A few examples of how things were before the cinema, the bingo hall and the television set took so much of the sparkle out of the life of the old town . . .

> Steeplechase week: Carmarthen will next week assume a gay appearance, as it generally does during the four or five days devoted to the annual steeplechases and the accompanying balls and hunts. A very large attendance of the County Families is anticipated, and fine weather alone is required to make the

Sanger's Circus passing through Nott Square in 1892. *(Mrs. Katie Evans).*

occasion go off with the usual éclat. Lists of acceptances would lead to the inference that the sport up at the course will be of the best kind, and there is every probability of tolerably large fields, whilst the quality of the horses that are likely to be present is a sufficient guarantee for the excellence of their running.

* * *

Band performance: On Saturday evening Mr. R. Marks's Brass Band played several popular tunes in Guildhall Square. The bandsmen took up their positions on the balcony of the Guildhall and played Handel's March 'Scipio'. This was followed by the Schottische 'Belle of the Ball', &c. &c., and the last item in the programme was the National Anthem. Mr. Marks and his coadjutors are to be complimented upon the excellence of their playing, which apparently was thoroughly appreciated by the large number of inhabitants assembled.

* * *

Jennings Theatre: This theatre has been open for the past ten days in the Market Place and is conducted in a most respectable manner by a talented company of actors and actresses, the entertainment, including plays ranging from high tragedy to low comedy, all being most creditably performed.

* * *

Vance in South Wales: Assembly Rooms, Carmarthen, for One Night Only: Under the Management of Mr. R. C. Leech, Vance's Concert Party: The novelty of all Mr. Vance's compositions is that they can be sung in any drawing room, the music being original and invariably pretty, and the words funny without being calculated to cause a blush.

Reserved seats 3 shillings [15p], family tickets to admit four 10 shillings [50p], front seats 2 shillings [10p], second seats 1 shilling [5p].

* * *

General Tom Thumb: Assembly Rooms, Carmarthen, Two Days Only—Grand Illuminated Morning Performance on

Saturday: General Tom Thumb, the smallest man in the world, 26 years old, well educated and not larger than a child of three years. In appearance he is a mere speck of humanity, but in intellect a giant. Has a remarkable versatility of talent and as a comedian, actor, singer and dancer has no equal. His songs, dances and impersonations cannot fail to please the most fastidious.

* * *

Star Theatre, Carmarthen: During the few months which Mr. John Noakes has been here with his theatre he has shown an amount of skill and enterprise in catering for public amusement which would do no discredit to managers whose good fortune had brought them far more favour and patronage in towns larger than ours. The performances have greatly varied in character and have all been carried out with a very fair regard to decorum as well as decency.

* * *

Assembly Rooms, Carmarthen: Last Two Nights of the Royal Comedy Drama Company. The Great London Comedy Pink Domino, as played in London and the provinces for over 2,000 nights, to conclude with the amusing farce Poor Pillicoddy. On the last night, the great Moral Temperance Drama 'Drink', at present playing to crowded houses at the Adelphi Theatre, London.

* * *

Assembly Rooms, Carmarthen: Great Attraction for Bank Holiday, for Two Nights only: Mr. D'Oyle Carte's Opera Company: On Monday Bank Holiday August 3rd—H.M.S. Pinafore; On Tuesday Princess Ida, written by W. S. Gilbert, composed by Arthur Sullivan. Plan of reserved tickets and seats at E. C. Evans, Stationery, Guildhall Square, Carmarthen.

* * *

The 9th Winter Evening Entertainment in aid of the Bridge Street and Towyside Schools was held at the Guildhall on Monday evening. Mr. William Spurrell, who occupied the chair, made a few appropriate remarks after which Messrs. C. & D. Jones'

String Band commenced the programme with a well-executed instrumental selection. Mr. Colby Evans followed with 'The Bosun's Story', which was loudly applauded.

* * *

Animated Photographs: There was an exhibition of Mr. David Devant's Animated Photographs at the Assembly Rooms. They include forty magnificent moving photographs of the most interesting character, and the entertainment includes some marvellous conjuring, ventriloquism, lightning cartooning, etc. The company, which by the by hails from the famous Maskellyne and Cooke's, of the Egyptian Hall, London, will also show tonight.

The keynote of those accounts of late-nineteenth century entertainments in Carmarthen was good taste and decorum. A far cry from the year 1848, when this account typified the behaviour of the 'lower orders' in the theatre:

Nigger Entertainment:[6] A person styling himself Mr. William Reed, who it will be remembered a short time ago was brought before the Borough Magistrates on a charge of stealing an umbrella, gave what he was pleased to term a Nigger Entertainment, and truly such a scene as presented itself it has not before been our fortune to witness.

The room was tolerably well filled (we will however say nothing of the respectability of the audience, but leave the few facts which we intend to give to speak for themselves). The self-styled Mr. William Reed having sung one or two songs, it was clear from certain evident signs that a 'storm was brewing', and they indeed were wise who took their departure before it burst, as it eventually did with relentless fury.

A few light hisses were the premonitory signs that something worse was coming, and when Mr. William Reed retired after dragging through one of the songs, a soldier (a great number of whose companions were present) took the stage and sang 'Mary Blane' in a far superior style to Mr. William Reed's performance. Reed, perceiving this, again got on the stage and most unceremoniously pushed his rival over, without even thanking him for his services.

The audience did not seem to relish this treatment, and shouts loud and long rent the air, amongst which now and then might be heard cries for the song 'The Lost Umbrella'—a most unmistakeable innuendo. A general melee then took place; whistling, shouting, jumping, fighting and a variety of other 'entertainments' ensued. Some persons wishing to see the fun climbed on the tops of the benches, which, in the confusion that prevailed, were overturned, precipitating their occupants into the middle of the row, and altogether such a scene took place as beggars all description.

The army patrol was sent for,[7] the police were called in, and at length something like order was restored. The programme was then proceeded with with a little 'Tumbling', a gentleman who rejoices in the cognomen of Flint being the performer, but having taken rather too much of the beverage that cheers and inebriates, he was not a very successful one, although his head was vastly inclined to come to the ground and stay there.

After this, some recitations were given, one of the soldiers repeating the speech of Brutus on the death of Caesar. When he came to that part 'Who's here so vile that he will not love his country?', he was answered by a youth nicknamed Nelson (on account of his having lost an eye, not by the fire of his country's enemies, but while engaged in a blacksmith's shop) who in a stentorian voice cried 'Me.' This roused the loyal feelings of the audience and he was set upon in right earnest and well pummelled, but it appeared that the poor fellow had suffered wrongfully, as he intended to have said that like his great namesake he *would* have died for his country.

Young Nelson then went through a variety of gambols, which were again followed by a regular row and no mistake, the Nigger, Reed, in vain calling for silence and for the first time appearing in the black and sombre hue of a genuine Nigger.

The affair terminated in riot and noise, and many were the curses levelled at the head of Mr. William Reed, who was characterised as an arrant imposter and one eminently deserving of the care and attention of the police.

As an appropriate finale, the services of the police were called in to oblige the 'Gentleman' to pay for the room—a proceeding which it appears he forgot to do!

No account of the contrasts and paradoxes in the lives of the people of nineteenth century Carmarthen would be complete without a look at the status of women, for here were contrasts galore. In 1865, for example, an imaginative piece of detective work by Sergeant David James of the Borough Police Force[8] provides a dramatic illustration of the moral outrage which then attended the discovery of the sin of adultery.[9] The

*Carmarthen Journal* headlined the story "Heartless Desertion of a Wife at Carmarthen" and went on to describe at great length how Thomas Hancocke, a guard on the Carmarthen and Cardigan Railway, a married man with five children, had eloped with a married woman with whom he had been enlivening his trips through Pencader, seven or eight miles down the line. She had come into "a considerable sum of money" and they set off for London, en route for the New York packet boat, sending their luggage ahead.

When the destitute Mrs. Hancocke applied for Parish Relief, the relieving officer acted quickly. He obtained a warrant from the magistrates and Sergeant James was sent off by train in hot pursuit. On the platform at Newport he found some boxes which he recognised as Hancocke's and which were labelled "John Titus—to be called for". Adopting the guise of a railway porter, Sergeant James met Mr. Titus when he came to collect the goods. It was not Hancocke, so, after the boxes were handed over:

> . . . the 'Porter' and his mates then requested 'John Titus' to stand a pot of ale, as was always the custom. To this the man complied, and the porters then in their turn stood pots of ale also, and after finishing him up with hot brandy they left him in the porters' room in the company of the 'Head Porter' [Sergeant James] who easily, with the help of the hot brandy, elicited the information that the boxes were to be received by 'Titus' of Newport and re-sent to Paddington under the same address, to be left till called for.
>
> This was done, and the officer started for Paddington also, where he concealed himself. When a man came and enquired for the goods, the clerk, feigning some excuse, desired him to call again at six in the evening. Sergeant James then quickly followed the man through the streets for about two miles, until in Praed Street, Paddington, he saw him go and speak to another man, whom he immediately recognised as Hancocke. The officer at once took him into custody and brought him to Carmarthen on the following day.

Hancocke's reception on his return to his home town shows vividly the contemporary attitude to this kind of thing, which in other circumstances would have led to him and his paramour being burned in effigy on the Ceffyl Pren.

> On arriving at the railway station, the fugitive was met by a

large concourse of women and children and was escorted through the town to the station house amidst tremendous hooting and yelling.

On Friday last he was brought before the Mayor and J. Rowlands Esquire, charged with deserting his wife and family, whereby they became chargeable to the Parish. He was fined £5.16s.4d. [£5.83p]. He was also committed to the House of Correction for two calendar months, the expense of his maintenance during his imprisonment to be defrayed out of the money found on him.

On the removal of the prisoner to the Gaol he was again surrounded by an eager but certainly not admiring crowd, who expressed their opinion of him in the most unmeasured and demonstrative forms. The fair sex especially were unusually prominent, and devoted their amiable energies to the task with more than usual perseverance.

The protective attitude towards women exemplified in this story is part of a complex set of attitudes prevailing in the nineteenth century—a counterbalance to woman's generally 'unliberated' status. The 'Fair Sex' did not have the vote, they owned nothing of the marital property and they were their husbands' chattels, in exchange for which—if they were of the middle or upper classes—they lived lives protected from everything that might offend their natural sensitivity and from every exertion that might overtax their physical delicacy. But if they were poor, they bore the brunt of just about everything that afflicted the poor. They bore large families, they scraped, scavenged and begged to feed and clothe them, and they made what comfort was possible in tiny, dark, ill-ventilated hovels. And being their husbands' chattels, they were subject to every drunken whim and brutality. Wife beating was rife. Eliza Lewis of Catherine Street told the magistrates a typical story:

'I was in Catherine Street and met my husband. I did not say a word to him, but he ran after me and asked me about some blankets. I ran into the house and he followed me and beat me about the arm with a stick. He often threatens me with a knife. I have sold a blanket belonging to the house. I did so because I had no food. He has beaten me before till I was black and blue and he has broken the bridge of my nose.'

After evidence was heard, Mr. Hughes, the Magistrate, said to the defendant 'Fortunately for you your wife has no legal corroboration of the fact that you beat her. She is black and blue and I have no doubt that you did beat her on this occasion and that you have done so many times before. Fortunately for you the case is not proved [!] and we are bound to discharge you. I am sorry for it, for I have no doubt that you did beat her.'

Defendant: 'I want to get rid of her, if you please. I can't live with her.'

Mr. Hughes: 'There are proper ways of getting rid of her without coming before us. Beating her is not the way to get rid of her, but if you continue doing so you may get rid of her in a way in which you will get rid of yourself too.

Quite so. The punishment for killing one's wife (as, of course, for killing anyone else) was death!

And an entry from the Borough Police 'Occurrence Book' for Monday night, the 30th of October, 1882:

Sergeant David Williams reports that shortly after half past ten o'clock this night he heard loud screams towards Cambrian Place and went to a yard and there saw Daniel Regan, an Irishman aged 23 years, beating his wife about the head. She also had hold of him. When separated, Regan was told to be quiet, but insisted he be locked up or one of them would be murdered. He then commenced to beat her again, when he was taken into custody and locked up. His wife's name is Bodicea Anne. The prisoner is a labourer and can read and write. No property on him.[10]

Every week, men charged with wife-beating trooped through the magistrates' court, but one domestic altercation at least had a somewhat different outcome, ending (as did most) with a reconcilliation . . . of a kind:

A Considerate Wife: The neighbourhood of the Quay of late is noted for quarrels between husbands and wives. On Thursday evening last, one of these little 'incidents' occurred and after a hot wrangling between the both, the husband in question threatened to drown his wife, who suddenly, to save her husband the trouble of drowning her as he threatened, made a leap over the quay into the river!

The first person that hurried to her rescue was the husband himself. Happily there was not much tide in at the time, otherwise there would be another tale to tell of this very considerate wife. How are all these would-be suicides escaping the notice of the authorities?

"A Bidding in good old Welsh fashion." *(National Library of Wales).*

But there *were* more assertive women about, such as the one whose wedding plans went slightly awry, an affair in which:

> The truth of the old saying 'There's many a slip between cup and lip' was strikingly illustrated in the experience of an intended bridal couple at Carmarthen. A young man from the neighbourhood of Pontyberem and a young woman from Crosshands met in Carmarthen in the morning for the purpose of sealing their vows. The young man was accompanied by his father, who brought a trap in which to take the happy couple to the bride's house where a bidding in good old Welsh fashion had been prepared.[11] All ran smoothly till Waterloo Terrace was reached on the way to the Workhouse, where the couple were to meet the registrar. At this point the bride, who seemed rather anxious, admonished her intended spouse to 'make haste.' This proved unfortunate, for the bridegroom took offence and stopped short and declared that he would go no further.
>
> Deaf to all entreaties he declared that his intended bride had developed into a missus too soon. He went back to town and spent the remainder of the day in a public house, where he celebrated his escape from the toils of matrimony by getting drunk, and towards evening his father took him home in a cart.

A Welsh Wedding. *(National Library of Wales).*

Returning from the wedding. *(National Library of Wales).*

The next day brought a calmer mood, and on Monday morning the bride and bridegroom again visited Carmarthen, presented themselves before the registrar, were made one . . . and together spend the day in the same public house which had afforded a refuge to the youth on the Saturday!

Women in pubs were not an uncommon sight, even in the male-dominated Carmarthen society of the 1800s, as the case of the two cockle ladies demonstrates:

> Eleanor Thomas and Anne Edwards, two cockle-ladies, were charged with being drunk and disorderly, assaulting the landlord of the Harp public house in Lammas Street,[12] and breaking his windows.
>
> The two defendants went into the Harp about ten o'clock at night, taking a jug of beer with them, on the principle of 'Carrying coals to Newcastle', and by way of diversion they commenced abusing the landlady and told her to go to a place not to be named to ears polite . . . but as the journey was very long and the place exceedingly warm, she declined.
>
> 'Mine Host' of the Harp, hearing their invitation, gave an intimation that their room would be more acceptable than their company. For this piece of gratuitous information Anne Edwards rewarded him with the contents of the jug slap bang in his face, asking him at the same time 'if he would have that', after which both of the prisoners demanded that the jug of beer should be replenished before they took their departure in peace.
>
> The demand not being complied with, Anne Edwards hit the landlord with a blow over the nose, after which the 'Ladies' gave tongue in a most approved Billingsgate fashion, when they were unceremoniously shown into the street and the door shut in their faces.
>
> No sooner was this effected than bang went one pane of glass and crash went another and the prisoners took to their heels with Police Constable [Henry] Fisher in full pursuit. But the chase was of short duration and the ladies of misrule were captured and confined to the cell.

That was only to be expected from cockle ladies, but consider the consternation in the town when a young lady of whom more decorum might have been expected rode through the streets of Carmarthen in what can only be described as an outrageously unorthodox manner:

What an eye-opener the people in Guildhall Square had shortly before nine o'clock on Thursday morning [1st September, 1892]. Coming down the Square, riding a well-fed mare, was a healthy, pleasant-looking young woman hailing from a farm about two miles away. Well, there is nothing unusual in that. No. But here is the joke: *she was riding astride!*

The Policeman on the beat was dumbfounded. He was doubtful whether he should prosecute the damsel for disturbing the public peace or allow her to proceed, with the hope that other female equestrians would follow her example.

A riding habit would have lessened the shock, but when a member of the Fair Sex rides astride without wearing . . . Ah! Well, she did ride astride, and there's an end of it.

And the old ladies in the town? Well, many of them liked to put themselves in the hands of the dependable 'Carmarthen Shilling' as a protection against bad luck:

Superstition in Carmarthen: Although we may be said to live in an age when witchcraft is generally disbelieved and when astrology is fast losing its hold, the relics of former credulities still linger. There is a prevalent opinion among certain classes in the town that it is unlucky and an unfavourable omen if ladies on first going out on New Year's Day happened to cast their eyes on one of the same sex as themselves. Nor is the idea a mere theme for sport or jest. It is firmly believed. Old women have actually engaged police officers to be their first visitors on New Year's Day in order to be favoured with good fortune during 1869!

They were, of course, superstitious women in a superstitious town, for Carmarthen was the place whose survival from flood, tempest and devastation depended upon the survival of . . . an Oak tree! None other than King Arthur's Wizard, Merlin, had—so legend told—tied Carmarthen's fate to the Oak tree that stood at the junction of Priory Street with Oak Lane. All knew the doom-laden words:

When Merlin's tree shall tumble down,<br>Then shall fall Carmarthen Town.

Hearts stopped beating in the town when, towards the end of the nineteenth century, an ill-disposed resident of Priory Street, driven to distraction by the noise of children playing around the tree, injected poison into it and killed it. But the

Cockle ladies on the sands at Ferryside: through the artist's eye, and through the camera's eye. *National Library of Wales).*

*(Mr. Roy Evans, Ferryside Residential Centre).*

Carmarthen's Old Oak at the end of the nineteenth century.
*(Mrs. Brenda Robinson).*

earth did not shake, the buildings did not fall and the waters did not rise, presumably because the tree had not exactly fallen, and catastrophe was kept at bay for the next seventy odd years by the shoring up of the Old Oak with a concrete support. Even when the dead tree became a hazard to motor traffic in the 1970s, plans to remove it caused mild panic in all parts of the town, including the inside of the hallowed walls of the Council Chamber . . . until the problem was solved by placing the withered stump under the protection of the Mayor himself. And there, in the foyer of Saint Peter's Civic Hall, safely within the town boundary, the Old Oak still stands as Carmarthen's sure defence against the fulfilment of Merlin's dire prophecy.

Strangely enough, though, it was from Carmarthen that a very much premature move came for votes for women:

> Women's Rights: The London papers have announced that Carmarthen's Member of Parliament has presented to the House of Commons a petition from this Borough in favour of extending the franchise to women.

All very commendable, but to say the least hardly in keeping with the views of his constituents. The real voice of male

''Catastrophe was kept at bay for the next seventy-odd years by shoring up the Old Oak with a concrete support''. *(Ken Davies, Mayfair Studios, Carmarthen).*

"In the foyer of St. Peter's Civic Hall, the Old Oak still stands as Carmarthen's sure defence against the fulfilment of Merlin's dire prophecy." *(The Town Clerk).*

Carmarthen was thundered by the *Carmarthen Journal* in response to this piece of news:

> Who Signed this Wonderful Document? It will be news to the 'Lords of Creation' in Carmarthen to know that the Fair Sex feel a total want of confidence in their political judgement. Is it desired that we should have a lady Member or Parliament as well as lady electors? We believe that this petition is really a sly radical move, done in secret because its promoters were afraid or ashamed to prosecute their canvass for signatures for it in the open day.
>
> At best it only represents the sentiments of a very feeble minority, and those a knot of sheer political agitators who delight in novelties. We recommend that a copy of it be framed for a museum of curiosities in the Carmarthen Literary Institute!

## NOTES

[1]The weaving trade was in particularly serious trouble, with fewer and fewer orders forcing masters to cut wages, which in turn caused strikes. In 1868, for example, there was a long and total 'lock-out' of weavers in the several Carmarthen mills in retaliation for the financial support they had sent to striking Swansea weavers.

[2]A quite startling exception to this statistic was found among the coraclemen, who were noted for their longevity (see *A Shilling for Carmarthen,* Chapter 8—'The Ebbing Tide').

[3]The Preliminary Report on the Sanitary Condition of the County of the Borough of Carmarthen, 1873, by John Hughes, F.R.C.S.

[4]See *A Shilling for Carmarthen,* Chapter 10—'An Army Vast, The Temperance Host'.

[5]Levelling out in 1873, wages and food prices remained stable for ten years or so afterwards.

[6]Nigger Minstrel Show, extremely popular in the U.S.A. and Britain at that time, in which the performers blacked their faces. B.B.C. Television's version of this style of entertainment was 'The Black and White Minstrel Show'.

[7]Many companies of troops were stationed in the town at the time, and the picquets patrolled the streets to keep order among them.

[8]Only six months later, in July, 1865, Sergeant James was drowned while swimming in the River Towy, along with Constable Evan Jones and an ex-Constable, William Powell. A concert organised for the benefit of the bereaved families was attended by nearly a thousand people.

[9]Another manifestation of public outrage against adulterers was the *Ceffyl Pren,* a riotous display of an adulterer in effigy. See *A Shilling for Carmarthen,* Chapter 4—'High Spirits and Wooden Horses'.

[10]Dyfed Archive Services—Museum Collection.

[11]A 'bidding' was the means of poorer couples obtaining goods and money with which to set up their first home on marriage. The word went around or an advertisement was put abroad that a wedding was to take place. All who came with presents were entertained with food and drink, and could be assured that when their time came they would get a present in return.

[12]Still open for business.

# TOWARDS THE THRESHOLD

The 'Good Old Days' are always seen through a veil that fickle memory draws over the bad times. In the 1870s, for instance, one "Old Inhabitant", pining for a slower pace of life long gone, remembered Carmarthen "in the olden days before the railway, fashionable headgear and the Saxon tongue displaced the coach, high black hat and the ancient language; when from evening parties ladies and gentlemen walked home escorted by maids and foot-boys carrying lanterns". We have seen enough of the quality of the lives of those who had no maids and foot-boys, and of the liberating influence of the railway age, to evaluate that warm and cosy image. It was perceived through memory's veil.

So, too, were the recollections years later of another "Old Inhabitant"—evidently an ex-policeman—who recorded his at a favourite time for such nostalgic excursions . . . the approach to the threshold of a new century. He had a "vivid recollection of the 'Good Old Days' of fifty years ago, when the Borough Police could live almost as comfortably on nine shillings [45p] as they can now on their present pay [£1 to £1.30p a week]". He went on to fond memories of butter at sixpence [2½p] a pound, cheese at three halfpence [less than 1p], choice cuts of beef and mutton twopence [1p], veal so cheap that "the best part of half a calf could be bought for little more than a shilling [5p]", a hundredweight of potatoes a shilling and eggs at seven for twopence [1p]. He remembered as many as forty-two carts standing in front of the Nag's Head Inn in Blue Street laden with large fresh herrings at eight for twopence [1p] and the cost of a "good big sewin" (sea trout) at a Groat [less than 2p]. His other recollections were equally warm and cosy.

And so are ours. When we are tempted to look back enviously on the 1p pint of milk, the 7p pound of butter and the 17½p shoulder of lamb of the first years of our own century, we are often blind to how great a portion those prices represented of the £1 or so a week on which the labourer and his large family had to live; how he began and ended his work in darkness, how short was his life expectancy, how hard his wife worked to scratch the barest of necessities for her children, how many of them died at birth or soon afterwards, how many of them succumbed to contagious diseases, and how ill-provided, damp, dark and crowded were the small houses they called home.

Carmarthen's "Old Inhabitant" was afflicted with the same human failing in the 1890s. He was right about the relationship between wages and prices, but if he had not been so afflicted he could have compared the "nightly riots and depredations" and the military interventions of his 'Good Old Days' with the quite different state of law and order in the streets of the 1890s, and the shuffling, shambling—almost furtive—perambulations of old Wil y Lôn of long ago with the ubiquitous presence of the 'Carmarthen Shilling' and the firm grip exerted by them on any who disturbed the peace. He could have recalled the distressed state of the families of the coraclemen whose hard-won sewin sold for only a Groat [fourpence, or less than 2p]. He could have compared the dreadful state of the town's drainage and water systems only twenty years before with the great strides towards the elimination of those death-traps reported year by year by Carmarthen's Medical Officer of Health. He could have compared Carmarthen's appalling death and child-mortality rates of 1873 with the improving state of the town's health, for while contagious and infectious diseases still appeared in the town at the rate of fifty or sixty cases a year, "Old Inhabitant" might have compared the five or six deaths a year of the 1890s with the forty or so of just twenty years before. And he might have considered the part played in this transformation by the smallpox vaccination programme which now kept pace with, and equalled, the town's birth-rate of a little over two hundred a year.

"Old Inhabitant" might also have thanked God he was alive. Twenty years before only one in six of the town's inhabitants died of old age. Now, as he penned his recollections, it was one in three.

The price of Carmarthen's great age as a town had been high in terms of the cost and effort required to sanify it and to cope with the decaying state of its most populous quarters. It is a problem that dogs the town to this day, but there has been nothing since to compare with the prodigious efforts and expenditure of the last thirty years of the nineteenth century. Medical Officer of Health, William Lewis Hughes, whose predecessor John Hughes had so shocked the town with his first review of its health problems in 1873, could report with justifiable satisfaction in 1900, the last year of the 19th century, that ". . . during the past years sanitation in Carmarthen has advanced by leaps and bounds, and when all the various schemes now in progress have been completed I am confident that the ancient Borough of Carmarthen will be able to hold its own with any town in the Principality when looked upon from a sanitary point of view".[1]

The streets had been transformed by the town's spanking new steamroller, purchased for £500, which now created conditions in which they were "much more sanitary than of old, the cleansing of them being greatly facilitated by their smooth and even surface''. Another pointer to the progress made since that year of 1873 when John Hughes had warned of the perils of digging the ground and letting loose the plague that lurked beneath, was his successor's report that ''all drains for new houses have now to be properly laid to the satisfaction of the Surveyor, jointed with cement and thoroughly tested before the houses can be occupied, and the Sanitary Inspector sees to the testing of all other new drains now coming under the provisions of the new By-Laws''. And he also reported what was perhaps the most significant development of the late nineteenth century in the field of public health and community life in Carmarthen—the provision (at a cost of about £5,000) of a park and recreation ground containing ''A magnificent cycle track of cement that is said to rival any track in England or Wales . . . with a view of attracting visitors to the town to witness cycle races and other sports''. The park and its amenities—still used for sports events and many other gatherings—was seen as ''an inestimable boon to the little children and rising generations of Carmarthen, who will now enjoy the privilege of possessing a fine open piece of land where they may at any time resort to pursue their games and pastimes, instead of being compelled to play in the streets,

Carmarthen's new park and cycle track, at the end of the nineteenth century.
*(Mrs. Anne Davies, Trevaughan).*

Carmarthen's cycling club poses before the Guildhall. *(Carmarthen Museum).*

exposed to the often times foul emanations proceeding from the open gratings of the sewers''. The Medical Officer of Health regarded it as ''one of the most important sanitary reforms that has been carried out in Carmarthen for many years'', coming as it did at a time when athletics, rugby football, ''round'' football, cycling and other sports were approaching a peak of popularity in the town, and a time when the local newspapers devoted more and more space to the activities of a generation nurtured through thirty years of compulsory elementary education that had turned most of them from the paths trodden by their less fortunate and less enlightened forefathers.

Compulsory elementary education may seem a far cry from what is available in the twentieth century, but it represented the next thing to a revolution in the way it transformed the morals, the ideals and the aspirations of millions.[2]

This was a Carmarthen very different from the 'Good Old Days'.

NOTES

[1]Carmarthen Sanitary Reports 1873-1899.

[2]The government contributed nothing towards the cost of education until 1833, when it made its first grant—£20,000—to the nation's educational charities. By 1900, thirty years after the introduction of compulsory elementary education, the State was contributing more than £10 million a year.

## The Flight of Industry

There were still problems, of course, and poverty was still endemic in some parts of the town, but the scale of it was a very far cry from the widespread destitution of the early part of the century, when starving wretches from the surrounding countryside and the mining villages stormed and ransacked the grain stores of the town, and when only the swords of the yeomanry cavalry kept the famished mobs from the decks of food-laden sailing ships alongside the quay. The plight of the poor was being aggravated now, though, by what was happening in the tinworks, the ironworks, the weaving sheds and other manufactories on which a substantial number of families still depended for a livelihood. Such industry as remained in the town was now in its death throes. For many years these ailing survivors of the industrial revolution had managed to give employment to a few hundred, but now, as the century approached its end, their time had come, and many of those who depended on them were being reduced to begging, charity or starvation. It was partly a reflection of the deep industrial depression in the Kingdom as a whole, for which a writer in 1882 had an explanation. If that explanation has a familiar ring about it in relation to our own times, we might ponder the view of the philosopher Hegel that "people and governments never have learned anything from history, or acted on principles deduced from it":[1]

> We held for many years a virtual monopoly of the mechanical appliances essential to industrial greatness. We made a vigorous use of our advantages; our commodities were cheap and good, and the world was satisfied to accept its supplies from us. We assumed it would always be so, and upon this theory we have accumulated on these islands vast aggregates of machinery and of labourers, for whom there could not possibly be found employment if foreign countries should undertake to manufacture for the supply of their own wants. But that is precisely what foreign countries have for many years been endeavouring, with much energy and success, to do.
>
> Our old outlets are failing us; our hopes must rest on the opening of new outlets, but the English manufacturer has a disabling confidence in the methods which heretofore have led him to success. He rejects novelties and is unwilling to be bored with experiments. In a world glowing with the love of progress and mechanical improvement, the mechanical conservatism of the English is undoubtedly the most perilous form of dry-rot by which our industrial system can be invaded."

But even allowing for this underlying malaise, the real cause —so far as Carmarthen was concerned—lay in the failure of old-established industries in towns remote from sources of raw materials to withstand the competition of techniques such as mass production now concentrated in the large manufacturing towns. The difficulties at Thomas, Lester's tinworks, where the workforce was halved in the last five years of the century, were compounded by a prolonged strike by the firm's two hundred workmen, a seemingly suicidal state of affairs brought about by a reduction in wages forced on an employer striving against all the odds to keep going. As the *Carmarthen Journal* saw it:

> The comparative isolation of the Carmarthen works from the coal and export centres militates greatly against their prosperity, and in fact it is only the personal influence of the firm [the Lesters, who lived in Carmarthen] which has kept them going so long, so that should the works be deserted by the present proprietors—which is now quite possible—the prospect of a restart will be remote.

This was in 1897. The tinworks survived the turn of the century by only a year.

So bad were things in Carmarthen's few industries towards the close of the century that the *Welshman* newspaper believed that "the regular beggars and loafers of the town" were too embarrassed to practise their craft in the face of the genuine plight of this normally hard-working section of the townspeople! Some indication of the scale of the problem can be gleaned from the proceedings of a meeting convened by the Mayor at the Guildhall for the purpose of considering what steps could be taken to mitigate the distress prevailing among the unemployed poor in the town. Chief Constable Thomas Smith, who with his men played a large part in the distribution of food and necessities to the needy, told the meeting that an increase in charitable donations had made it possible to supplement the work of the well-established soup kitchen for the poor by the distribution of some 350 loaves each day. The Mayor told the audience that in Priory Street alone over the past fourteen days nine hundred meals had been provided for the poor children of the town, and one kind lady, Mrs. R. M. Thomas, had been giving free breakfasts to poor children, the Mayor being present on one occasion to see three hundred little ones enjoying her benevolence.

And yet, though unemployment benefit was still over a decade away[2] and the 'Welfare State' as we know it some half a century, only the most helpless of the displaced workers would suffer the indignity, the "disgrace", of "going on the Parish" by seeking relief in the Workhouse or as "Outdoor paupers". There was a fierce pride among these people and a close-knit neighbourliness that assured a helping hand from

A busy and prosperous town, with livestock fairs second to none. "John Brown's" Fair in Guildhall Square and Lammas Street at the end of the nineteenth century. *(Emlyn Jones).*

neighbours equally afflicted whenever death, hunger or privation visited the poor quarters of the town. Perhaps the nineteenth century, with all its imperfections, is not entirely devoid of some kind of lesson for we sophisticates of the twentieth century.

What the displaced workers and their families could not know was that the industrial problems which brought about their hardships were really an element of a fundamental social change . . . the 'withdrawal symptoms' associated with Carmarthen's reversion to its natural role as an agricultural market town. Harrowing as is this picture, then, it must be seen in that context, because most people could find employment in the offices and shops, in the hotels and inns, in the markets and the stables, on the railways and with the hauliers, and as domestic servants, though hours were long and the reward hard-earned. But it was work, and work gave people pride, dignity and the urge to better themselves. Furthermore, trade was good and those who conducted the town's commercial life prospered accordingly—their fine new houses, their chintz-curtained, antimacassared, moralistic and charitable lifestyles reflecting the solid achievements of the Victorian middle-class.

The County Gentry still visited the town in their fine carriages: A carriage waits by Saint Peter's Church. *(Carmarthen Museum).*

And the 'County Gentry', though far less powerful than sixty years before when their dynastic combinations treated Carmarthen as a private political arena, still evoked the awe and forelock-touching respect of the common inhabitants whenever they visited the town for a society wedding, a hunt ball, an agricultural show or the annual horse races; their carriages and their fine apparel still brought a special elegance to the crowded streets and ageing architecture of the old town. But these were their twilight years, for their country estates and their accustomed lifestyles would—sooner than any of them could have dreamed—fall victim to a novel and seemingly modest idea in revenue raising introduced in 1894. To-day we know it as death duties!

## NOTES

[1] *The 19th Century—A History,* Robert Mackenzie, (T. Nelson & Sons, London, 1882).

[2] David Lloyd George, the outstanding reformer of the Liberal government, was largely responsible for the introduction of National Health and Unemployment Insurance in 1911.

## What Strides

And so, with this infinite variety of people and activity, the picture presented to the visitor to Carmarthen at the end of the nineteenth century was of a busy and prosperous town with well-stocked shops catering for every taste and income, with livestock marts and fairs second to none in the Principality, with a large and thriving provision market drawing buyers and sellers from far and wide, with bustling streets and crowded pubs filled with people who seemed to be enjoying life.

Today we may be justifiably impressed by the rapid rate of social and technological progress that this century has seen, and believe that there has been no other like it. But has there not?

If mobility, communications and literacy are the keys to whatever the world may look like to-day, who can deny that the break-through in all of them occurred during the nineteenth century, to provide the base on which all else has been built? Consider a few examples as they affected Carmarthen:

In 1800 it took nearly a fortnight, if conditions were very good (and the roads were virtually impassable during the winter months) for goods to travel from London to Carmarthen by horse waggon, and at best four days to travel from an all but isolated Carmarthen to London by stage coach, at a cost far beyond the reach of all but the 'upper classes'. In 1860, by railway, at fares within the reach of thousands of ordinary people, it took six hours. Now, a hundred and twenty years later, it takes four hours.

In 1800 a two-month voyage to America by sailing ship was by no means exceptional, and news from that continent travelled at just that speed. In 1900 the many hundreds of emigrants from Carmarthenshire could do the crossing by steamship in about five days—hardly different from the speed of the last British transatlantic liner, Queen Elizabeth II in the 1970s—and messages could be tapped out along a transatlantic telegraph cable.

In 1800 there were no seagoing steam-boats, and only the French were experimenting with a rudimentary river steam paddler. Only thirty-eight years later a steam ship had crossed the Atlantic Ocean.

In 1805 the news of Nelson's victory at Trafalgar, 650 miles away, reached Carmarthen by sailing ship and stage coach twenty-three days after the event. In 1900 it took the same time for a letter written by Carmarthen volunteer Johnny Phillips to travel the 7,000 miles by horse waggon, railway train and steamship from a remote battle front in South Africa to his friends at the *Carmarthen Journal* Office. To-day's air mail might take up to a third of that time. But in 1800 a young man like Johnny Phillips would in all probability have been unable to write a letter anyway. He would more likely than not have been totally illiterate and have had no schooling of any kind. In 1900 every child in the Kingdom went to school and acquired at least a basic literacy and numeracy. But now, as Britain enters the 1980s, the word 'scandal' is being applied to the alleged widespread decline in just such basic educational achievements!

In 1800 a handful of people decided the shape of national

and local government, and a town that had the misfortune to be the scene of a contested election might just as well be under war-time siege. By the end of the century all the signs were that universal suffrage would not be long in coming, and the election proceedings themselves—thirty years after the introduction of the secret ballot—were mercifully free of militia bayonets and cavalry sabres.

In 1800 more than two hundred crimes attracted the death penalty and Assize calendars were full of such sentences for trivial thefts, such was the power of property. For nearly half the century prison ships plied the seas between Britain and her colonies in Australasia, carrying thousands who would never see their homeland again for crimes which to-day would call for a small fine. By the century's end the death penalty remained only for treason, murder and piracy with violence, and transportation had long ceased to feature in the penal system.

In 1800 the masses dwelt in a pit of ignorance and privation from which their established church did little to lift or encourage them. By 1900, through the influence of Nonconformism, religion had returned to the people and its effect on social progress was profound. As the century closed, Carmarthen was about to give that influence a substantial boost. It was there that the Rev. W. S. Jones of Penuel Chapel was experiencing the stirrings that within two or three years would lead to his "Visitation from the Lord"—that "Indelible consciousness of the amazing Holiness of God—like a purifying fire—like a fiery river flowing out of the throne"[1] that would spur the Great Welsh Religious Revival of 1904. He (through the revelation he would receive at Loughor) and other preachers like W. W. Lewis of Carmarthen Presbyterian Church, Professor Ceri Evans of Priory Street Chapel, Josuah Jenkins, Seth Joshua and Evan Roberts, who were seeking through their pulpits and through cottage prayer meetings a break from uninspiring religious orthodoxy, would find that new expression of the Gospel which was to take south and west Wales by storm. Between them they would bring about "the change from Judgement Preaching to a message of love and compassion, opening the floodgates and releasing all the spiritual forces from their long bondage to formality and cold orthodoxy".[2]

The impact of the revival in Carmarthen would be profound, and its effect long-lasting. It would catch the imagination of the people and add momentum to the process of social change and enlightenment in the town, and it would be one of the great civilising influences.

There was still far to go in the march towards the bridging of class divisions and the goal of the egalitarian society, but the direction was being clearly sign-posted and the road being firmly laid. Looking at other sign-posts along this road, and following the current fashion for reviewing the state of the nation at the threshold of the twentieth century, the *Carmarthen Journal* printed its own "Retrospect of the nineteenth Century and its Social Reformation":

> A great change has gradually taken place in the manners and customs of the people during the nineteenth century. Certainly we have changed for the better. In the early years of the century there was much that was coarse and brutal in every grade of society. It is said that the character of a nation may be told from its amusements. We may therefore form an estimate of the early nineteenth century when we read of cock-fighting, bull-baiting and prize fighting [they might have added public hangings] which were the chosen delights of the people.
>
> Before the advent of the school boards the lower orders were hopelessly ignorant, and before the growth of railways communication was so difficult that the people were governed by a narrow patriotism that made them regard every outsider with contempt and hatred.[3] In the upper classes duelling was of frequent occurrence and many brave lives were lost over some petty squabble not worth putting hand to sword hilt. Another evil which cankered the heart of the nation was gambling. Even now this evil exists, but to nothing like the extent as in the early nineteenth century, when noblemen mortgaged their estates, women ruined their husbands, husbands left their wives destitute as the result of their passion.

And, inevitably in any assessment of nineteenth century social behaviour in Carmarthen, one aspect called for special mention:

> Even the Demon Drink, rampant as it still is, is restricted more

"In 1900 every child in the Kingdom went to school and acquired at least a basic literacy and numeracy": Quay Street School. *(Carmarthen Museum).*

to the lower sections of society and does not flaunt in high places. Even as late as Dickens' time we read of gentlemen sitting late over their bottles until they fell beneath the tables or were carried speechless to bed, and this was regarded with good humoured indulgence as a characteristic appertaining to a good station in life, and something to be smiled at but not blamed. Things have changed. Nowadays a gentleman who would fall asleep under the table, or enter a drawing room the worse for liquor would quickly be shown the door.

In this brief sketch it is impossible to draw a detailed picture of social life in the early and latter part of the century, but the verdict may be given that on the whole the people are more refined, more intellectual and more virtuous than their forefathers.

They were . . . but there was life in the old town yet. Nearly eighty years later, its ministers of religion would still be lamenting Carmarthen's image as a drinkers' town. They raised a veritable storm of protest when (in 1977) the *Western Mail* reported a generous extension by the town magistrates for over a hundred pubs . . . under the headline 'Welsh Drinkers' Paradise'.

Clearly, though, there had been great strides. And there were great strides at hand. The first motor car had been driven into Carmarthen, and the town would soon have its first telephone. Marconi was about to span the Atlantic Ocean by radio, and already men far away were building the first flying machines. In less than twenty years aeroplanes would be delivering letters right into Carmarthen! Royal Air Force biplanes made regular flights into Carmarthen in September and October, 1919, delivering mail bags which would otherwise have been held up by a rail strike.

Yes, Carmarthen—and, to be fair, the rest of the world—entered the twentieth century from a powerful springboard.

## NOTES

[1]W. S. Jones' own words—from his diary.

[2]A newspaper comment of that time.

[3]In Wil y Lôn's day towns were still under the old 'Watch and Ward' law of 1285, and in all but the closing of the town gates Carmarthen was shut off from a hostile outside world when the sun set. Strangers would as likely as not find themselves brought to account before the magistrates, and old Shôn Dwr would tie the undesirables among them to the tail of his cart and whip them as they were dragged to the borough boundary!

# INDEX


| | *A Shilling for Carmarthen* | *Four Cheers for Carmarthen* |
|---|---|---|
| Army (local volunteer units): | | |
| Carmarthen Volunteers | | 4, 21, 135, 170 |
| Carmarthenshire Militia | 13, 15, 21, 30, 34-37, 123 | 14, 20, 96, 136, 148 |
| Carmarthenshire Yeomanry | 130 | 136 |
| Castlemartin Yeomanry | | 82 |
| Chelsea Pensioners (reservists resident in Carmarthen) | 72, 74, 75 | 148 |
| Royal Carmarthenshire Artillery Militia | | 36, 170 |
| Royal Carmarthenshire Fusiliers | | 8, 20 |
| Royal Carmarthenshire Rifle Militia | | 28 |
| Welch Regiment (41st) 1st Volunteer Bn. | 186, 187 | 36, 38 |
| Assembly Rooms | 111, 117, 155, 182, 183, 190 | 84, 166, 169, 172, 180-4 |
| Assizes | 119 | |
| Banks | 105 | 141 |
| Battles and Wars: | | |
| Alma (Crimean War) | | 32, 34 |
| Badajoz (Peninsular War) | | 6, 7, 14 |
| Balaclava (Crimean War) | | 36, 42 |
| Colenso (Boer War) | | 42, 52 |
| Drieburg (Boer War) | | 43 |
| Inkerman (Crimean War) | | 32 |
| Kabul (Afghan Wars) | | 22 |
| Paardeburg (Boer War) | | 43, 53 |
| Salamanca (Peninsular War) | | 20 |
| Spion Kop (Boer War) | | 40, 42 |
| Trafalgar | | 2-4 |
| Vittoria (Peninsular War) | | 14, 20 |
| Waterloo | | 11-13, 14, 20, 21, 42 |
| Bidding | 117 | 189 |
| Boer War | 193 | 37-58 |
| Boer War, Letters from | | 42, 43-44, 45-47, 50-54 |
| Brothels | 100, 102, 116 | |
| Cambrian (Newspaper) | | 132 |
| Capital punishment | | 137, 209 |
| Carmarthen Borough Police Force (see 'Police') | | |
| Carmarthen Journal | | 132 |
| 'Carmarthen Justice' | 22, 25, 26, 40, 41, 42, 46 | |
| 'Carmarthen Mob' | 4, 10, 14, 15, 23, 37, 78, 86, 110, 194 | 90 |
| Ceffyl Pren | 61, 62, 65, 91, 130, 160, 162, 163 | 186, 197n. |
| Celebrations: | | |
| Boer War, departure of Carmarthen volunteers | | 44-5 |
| Boer War, Monument, dedication | | 56 |
| Boer War, return of volunteers | | 55-6 |
| Crimean War, ending | | 31 |
| Crimean War, return of Doctor Lawrence | | 32 |
| First paddle steamer at Carmarthen | | 97-8 |
| Fusilier Monument, dedication | | 32 |

| | *A Shilling for Carmarthen* | *Four Cheers for Carmarthen* |
|---|---|---|
| Mafeking, relief of | | 47-9 |
| Napoleon, abdication | | 8 |
| New Year's Eve, 1800 | 7 | |
| New Year's Eve, 1900 | 196, 197 | |
| Nott, Sir William, return from India | | 24-6 |
| Picton Monument, dedication (1828 and 1846) | | 13-17 |
| Picton, Sir Thomas, return from Peninsular | | 7-8 |
| Prince of Wales, marriage | | 169, 171-2 |
| Queen Victoria, Coronation | | 148-9 |
| Queen Victoria, Diamond Jubilee | 186, 189 | |
| Queen Victoria, Proclamation | | 148 |
| Railway, opening of line to Carmarthen | | 74-8 |
| Trafalgar, battle of | | 2-4 |
| Chapels | 5, 196 | 140, 144 |
| Charter Day (elections) | 34, 35, 39, 42, 44, 45 | |
| Chelsea Pensioners (see 'Army') | | |
| Christmas Eve | 61, 111, 130, 155 | |
| Cockle Ladies | | 144, 191 |
| Colleges (see 'Schools and Colleges') | | |
| Commerce and Industry, state of | 5, 6, 143 | 132, 141-2, 144-5, 153-4, 172-3, 177-8, 202-4 |
| Coracles and Coraclemen | 8, 23, 24, 91, 92, 93, 102, 112, 125-140 | 16, 134, 144, 170, 171, 179 |
| Corporal punishment | 120 | |
| Corruption, municipal | 9, 12, 45 to 48 | |
| Death rate | 126 | 132, 146, 161, 175, 199 |
| Drunkenness | 8, 97, 110 | 210-1 |
| Duelling | 33 | 210 |
| Education | 97, 111, 134 | 105, 106, 137, 144, 149, 168, 171, 202, 208 |
| Elections | 111 | |
| Elections, Influence of 'County' families | 14 | |
| Elections, Reform (April 1831) | 15-21 | |
| Elections, Reform (August 1831) | 26-35 | |
| Electoral Reform | 4, 12-37 | 136, 208-9 |
| Emigration | | 110, 124-5, 147 |
| Employment, conditions | | 153-4, 204-5 |
| Employment, Wages | | 179 |
| Entertainments | 6, 95, 96, 111 | 180-5, 210 |
| Fairs | 96, 191, 192 | 207 |
| Fire Brigade | 166-172 | |
| Food, prices | | 135, 145, 165, 179, 198 |
| Food, Riots | | 135 |
| Food, Shortage | | 135 |
| Furnace House | 192 | 10, 138 |
| Fusilier Monument | 118, 193, 194 | 32, 170 |
| Gaols (Borough and County) | 5, 6, 22, 23, 41, 43, 47, 86, 101, 102, 104, 129, 144, 146-153, 199 | 140, 146, 186-7 |

| | *A Shilling for Carmarthen* | *Four Cheers for Carmarthen* |
|---|---|---|
| Hangings | 5, 6, 7, 146-153 | |
| Health and Hygiene | 107 | 132, 141, 145, 150, 153, 156-63, 175-6, 199-200 |
| Home Office | 20-25, 34, 41, 48, 64, 151 | |
| Horse Races | | 143, 180-1 |
| Hotels (see 'Public Houses') | | |
| Housing | 8 | 132, 138-40, 157-8, 177 |
| Industry (see 'Commerce and Industry') | | |
| Inns (see 'Public Houses') | | |
| Irish immigrants | 110, 118 | 155-7 |
| Iscoed | | 8, 10 |
| Literary and Scientific Institution | 111, 182, 183 | 166, 180 |
| Lodging houses | 141, 155 | |
| London Metropolitan Police | 4, 12, 26-31, 33-37, 48, 52, 53, 82 | |
| Market, livestock | 191 | 165-6, 169 |
| Markets, old | 6, 97 | 136, 140, 163 |
| Markets, new | 191 | 77, 83, 163-6, 171, 173, 174 |
| Merthyr S.S. | 190 | 126 |
| Municipal Corporations Act, 1835 | 48, 55 | |
| Nott Monument | 192 | 26-7, 45 |
| Old Oak | | 192-4 |
| Park and cycle track | | 200 |
| Parliamentary Commission on Municipal Corporations in England and Wales, 1834 | 19, 42, 45-48, 52 | 107,114 |
| Paxton's Tower | 13 | |
| Picton Monument | | 11, 13-14, 17-18, 138, 148, 170, 171 |
| Police: | | |
| Carmarthen Borough Force, creation of | 2, 50-54 | |
| Carmarthen Borough Force, end of | 1, 2 | |
| Chief Constables | 1, 2, 16, 17, 18, 20, 31, 33, 39, 44, 47, 48, 51-58, 60, 69, 84, 86, 87, 88, 92, 101, 142 | |
| Disciplinary problems | 55-60, 88, 89, 90, 102, 115, 116, 117, 142 | |
| Duty diaries and occurrence books, extracts from | 112-118, 134-139, 141, 154-168 | 169, 188 |
| Station, Cambrian Place | 1, 2, 3, 191, 199 | 174 |
| Population | 5 | 132, 138, 175 |
| Post Office | | 63, 64 |
| Poverty and poor relief | 8, 110, 195 | 134-5, 138, 145, 146, 150-1, 172-5, 204 |
| Prostitutes | 43, 56, 98-102, 120, 121, 136 | |

| | *A Shilling for Carmarthen* | *Four Cheers for Carmarthen* |
|---|---|---|
| Public Houses, Inns and Hotels: | | |
| Angel | 112, 117 | |
| Angel Inn (Cardigan) | | 63 |
| Belle Vue (Aberystwyth) | | 66 |
| Boar's Head | 6, 7, 21, 27, 111, 167, 193, 197 | 3, 17, 63, 97, 142, 143, 150 |
| Boat | 137 | |
| Boat and Anchor | 158 | |
| Buffalo | 190 | |
| Bull and Mouth (London) | | 61 |
| Castle | | 141 |
| Castle (Brecon) | | 60 |
| Cawdor Arms (Newcastle Emlyn) | 170 | |
| Ceffyl Du | 93, 199 | |
| Coburg Hotel (Tenby) | | 97 |
| Coopers Arms | 115, 116 | 33 |
| Cressely | 94 | |
| Emlyn Castle | 163 | |
| Golden Keys | 104 | |
| Half Moon | | 3, 142 |
| Hare | 43 | |
| Harp | | 33, 191 |
| Horse and Jockey | 190 | |
| Ivy Bush | 27, 32, 80, 155 | 2, 3, 4, 10, 16, 21, 55, 61, 63, 64, 66, 77, 141, 143 |
| Jolly Tar | 125 | 92, 129, 144 |
| King's Arms | | 151 |
| King's Head | 137 | |
| Lamb | | 114 |
| Lion Royal | | 72 |
| Mansel Arms | 199 | |
| Mariners Arms (Ferryside) | | 73 |
| Marquis of Granby | 59 | |
| Morgans Arms | 68 | 138 |
| Nag's Head | | 3, 142, 198 |
| Nelson | | 140 |
| Old Plough | 150 | |
| Pelican | 137, 190 | |
| Plough | 163 | |
| Plough and Harrow | 73, 76, 77 | |
| Queen's Hotel | 192 | |
| Railway Inn | 137, 190 | |
| Railway Tavern | 188 | 70 |
| Red Cow | 190 | |
| Red Lion Inn | | 3, 142 |
| Royal Exchange | 90 | |
| Ship | 132 | |
| Ship and Castle | 165 | |
| Six Bells | | 146 |
| Smiths Arms | | 148 |
| Star and Garter | 39, 40 | |
| Talbot Inn | | 3, 142 |
| Tanners Arms | 191, 199 | |
| Three Salmons | 165 | |
| Vine | 118, 154 | |
| Weavers Arms | 199 | |
| Wheatsheaf | 190 | |

| | *A Shilling for Carmarthen* | *Four Cheers for Carmarthen* |
|---|---|---|
| Races (see 'Horse Races') | | |
| Railway: | | |
| – Accident, first in Carmarthen | | 80-2 |
| – Bridge over River Towy (White Bridge) | | 82, 110 |
| – Carmarthen, opening of line to | 107, 109 | 74-78, 84, 85 |
| – Construction, Swansea to Carmarthen line | | 71, 73-4 |
| – Excursions | | 71, 72, 78, 80, 82, 83, 84 |
| – Freight train, first into Carmarthen | | 74 |
| – Haverfordwest, opening of line to | 109 | 82 |
| – Navvies, riots at Ferryside | 108 | 73 |
| – Services | | 78, 80, 208 |
| – Ship connections | | 109 |
| – Stage coach connections | | 64, 66, 68 |
| Rebecca Riots | 62-85, 126 | |
| Rebecca Riots, Carmarthen invasion of | 75-79 | |
| Rebecca Riots, Fourth Light Dragoons, charge of | 80, 81 | 34, 35 |
| Rebecca Riots, Talog ambush | 72-75 | |
| Rebecca Riots, Water Street Gate | 67-72 | |
| Rebecca Riots, Workhouse, attack on | 79, 80, 81 | |
| Reform (see 'Electoral Reform') | | |
| Religious Revival | 134 | 209, 210 |
| Riot Act | 40 | 154n |
| Riots: | | |
| – Charter Day, 1831 | 36, 37 | |
| – Charter Day, 1832 | 39, 40 | |
| – Cheese, 1818 | | 136 |
| – Colliers, 1801 | | 136 |
| – Ferryside, railway navvies | 108 | 73 |
| – Fishermen, 1831 | 23, 24 | |
| – Press Gang, 1803 | | 90 |
| – Reform (April 1831) | 12-37 | |
| – Reform (August 1831) | 28-34 | |
| Sabbath, profaning | 102, 103 | |
| Saint David's Church | | 20, 105 |
| Saint Peter's Church | 5, 7, 33, 34, 112, 119, 181, 192, 197 | 3, 13, 24, 26, 31, 32, 135, 138, 148, 162, 174 |
| Schools and Colleges: | | |
| – Charity Schools | | 105 |
| – Elementary Schools | 134 | |
| – Grammar Schools | | 166 |
| – Lancastrian Schools | 97, 111 | 168 |
| – Presbyterian College | | 168 |
| – Royal Free Schools | | 144 |
| – Sunday Schools | 111, 134 | 105, 106, 144, 149, 171 |
| – Teacher Training College | | 168, 171 |
| Shipping: | | |
| – Bristol Steam Navigation Company | | 97, 103, 107, 109, 110, 114-7 |
| – Emigration | | 110, 124, 125, 147 |
| – Excursions | | 104-6, 123 |
| – Pockett, Mr., Swansea shipowner | | 117, 119 |
| – Railway connections | | 109 |
| – Stage coach connections | | 96-7 |
| – Trade, state of | 5 | 91, 92, 101-4, 107, 108, 114-7, 126-7 |

| | *A Shilling for Carmarthen* | *Four Cheers for Carmarthen* |
|---|---|---|
| Ships: | | |
| Last at Carmarthen | 125 | 129 |
| Launchings | | 92, 93, 113-4, 118-9 |
| Steamship, first to visit Carmarthen | | 97, 98 |
| Shipwrecks | | 94, 98, 100, 120-3 |
| Smugglers | | 106, 107 |
| South African War (see 'Boer War') | | |
| Special Constables | 17, 18, 20, 23, 24, 26, 27, 28, 31, 35, 37, 72, 109 | |
| Stage Coaches, accidents | | 69-71 |
| Stage Coaches, Railway connections | | 65-8 |
| Stage Coaches, Railway, impact of | | 78, 80 |
| Stage Coaches, Services | | 60, 61, 62, 64, 65, 66, 208 |
| Stage Coaches, Ship connections | | 96-7 |
| Stocks | 6 | 140, 163 |
| Suicide | 103 | |
| Sunday drinking | 93, 119, 165, 176, 177 | |
| Superstition | 154 | 192, 194 |
| Temperance movements | 96, 97, 174-184 | |
| Theatre | 111 | 144, 182-4 |
| Torch Night (see 'Christmas Eve') | | |
| Transportation, penal | 105 | 137, 209 |
| Turnpike roads | | 60-3 |
| Wars (see 'Battles') | | |
| Watch and Ward (see 'Watchmen') | | |
| Watch Committee | 48, 51-60, 72, 74, 84, 87-91, 101, 142, 171, 172, 190, 191 | |
| Watchmen | 3, 4, 8, 9, 10, 16 48, 51, 53, 123 | 4, 210 |
| White Bridge | | 82, 110 |
| Wide Ocean, The | | 140, 144, 163 |
| Women, status of | | 185-96 |
| Workhouse | 66, 67, 79-82, 105, 120, 126 | 34, 35, 140, 156, 159, 171, 173 |
| Wreckers (Dynion y Bwyelli Bach—'The men of the little axes') | | 96, 120, 122 |

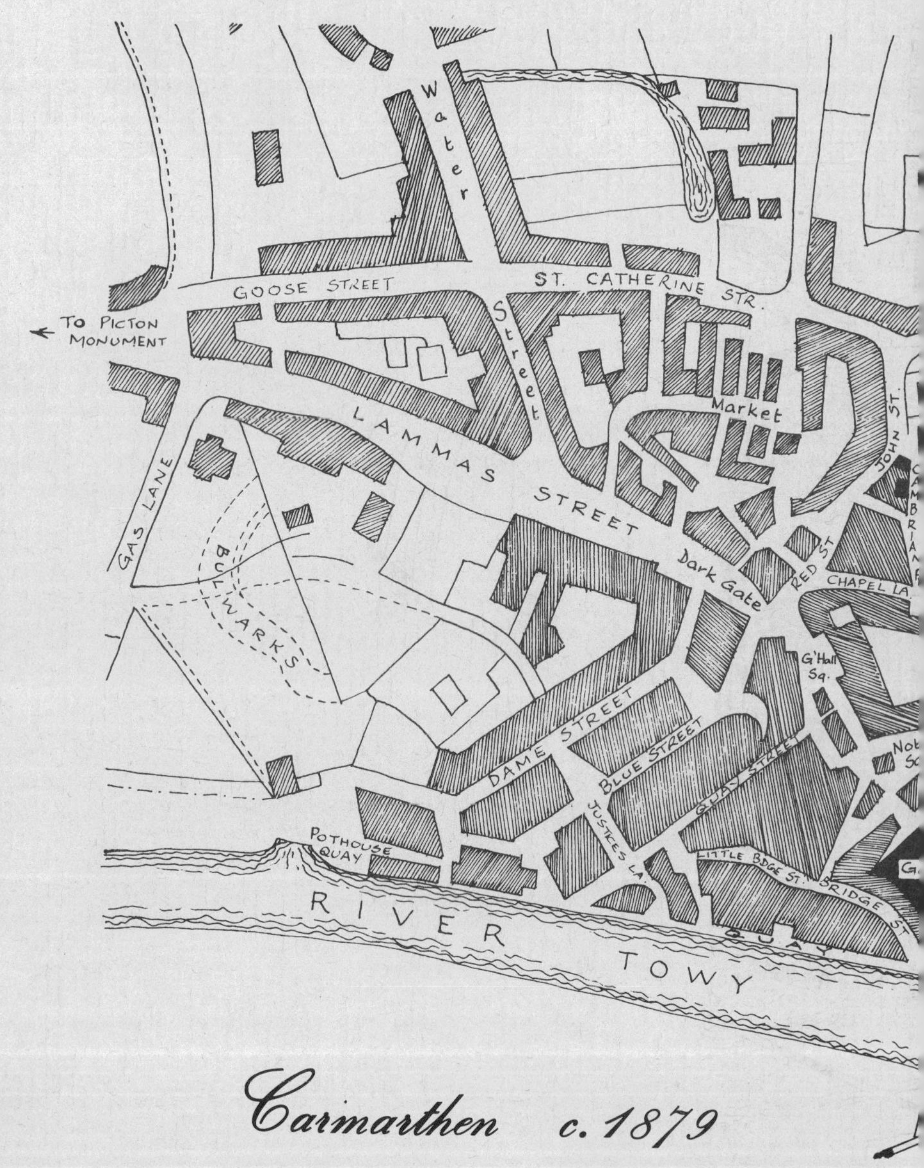


*Carmarthen c. 1879*